Pioneer

Free Will Baptists

Ministers

Burial Locations

In

New Hampshire

This book was printed in the United States of America.

To order additional copies of this book, contact:
FWB Publications
Enchanting Acres
1006 Rayme Drive
Columbus, Ohio 43207
Alton.loveless@prodigy.net
Or
www.amazon.com

FWB
FWB Publications

Introduction

New Hampshire

This book represents all that were part of the Free Will Baptist movement, consisting of the Palmer (south), Randall (north) and others such as the Stone, John-Thomas, John Wheeler Assns., NC OFWB and more.

Many of the photos are poor quality, but it was all I could find. Likewise, I do not have photos or tombstones for many of them. The information about these ministers were all that was available to me or found in archives. I made every effort to include those for which they would be remembered. Some I had no information, but research had shown they were of our denomination.

This Section is taken for a two Volume set done by this author.

New Hampshire

Austin Wakefield Avery
Birth:
Nov. 18, 1838
Campton
Grafton County, New
Hampshire
Death:
Oct. 5, 1865
Haverhill
Essex County,
Massachusetts
Burial:
Blair Cemetery
Campton
Grafton County, New
Hampshire

At 16 he took a public stand for Christ in revival. He entered the New Hampton Institution to prepare for the ministry in 1856. Two years later he was licensed to preach. Shortly after he went to Paducah, Kentucky in early 1859 to visit his brother and to make a tour through nine of the southern states and saw slavery as it was. He returned to Dover, New Hampshire to supply for three months. And 51 requested interest in Christian prayers. For a while he served as an agent of the New York City church raising funds for building. When a revival broke out where he had settled. He resigned that job and settled in Parishville, where he was ordained at the age of 21 on March 24, 1860. In January 1861 he went to Boston to study with Rev. Ransom Dunn and on March 13 he became pastor of the Boston church. Through his four years of pastorate, a great interest continued till 1865 had been added to the church 156 of them by baptism. With the ministry of only six years he baptized 175, when an illness overtook him and he died in his 27th year. He was buried in his native state with the funeral being preached by Dr. Isaac the Stewart. Note: Additional information from *Native Ministry of New Hampshire.*

J. Franklin Babb
Birth:
May 20, 1873
New Hampshire
Death:
May 31, 1938
Laconia
Belknap County, New Hampshire
Burial:
New Hampton Village Cemetery
New Hampton
Belknap County, New Hampshire
Plot: 165

His parents were John W. Babb and Josephine H. (Damon) BABB. Was married to Candace Porter Ladd, 11 Oct. 1897, at Ladd's Hill,

Belmont, NH. She was the dau of Arthur S. Ladd and Ellen M. (Porter) LADD. Rev. Babb was fondly called "the sporting parson" by editors and those who knew his affinity for the outdoors and his hunting and fishing expeditions. He was often called upon by groups to speak as he always drew a crowd for his entertaining way of presenting his subject. He was the last pastor of the New Hampton Freewill Baptist church, before it became the New Hampton Community church after 1911. It was originally built as a Freewill Baptist church in the 1800's and is now on the National Registry of Historic places.He pastored for some years in Mass. before the last one at New Hampton.

Wm. S Babcock
Birth:
Nov. 15, 1764
Death:

Aug. 29, 1821
Burial:
Babcock-Cate Cemetery,
Barrington,
Strafford County,
New Hampshire

Son of a wealthy merchant, who sent him to Yale College to prevent his being drafted as a soldier. After school, he settled in Springfield, VT, where he began a study of the Scripture to refute its teachings. But it mightily convinced him of its truth, and he was converted in 1800, and at once began to preach. Becoming acquainted with the Freewill Baptists, he found himself in agreement with them, was baptized and ordained by Rev. Jeremiah Ballard of NH. He gathered a church together, of 25 members, sent a letter to the Quarterly Meeting requesting instruction and fellowship, whereupon another church under Rev. Stephen Place, joined with Rev. Babcock's church and were in fellowship. These were pioneer days for the church in Vermont. Rev. Wm. Babcock and Nathaniel Marshall, convinced Rev. John Colby, the young FWB Vermont evangelist, to be ordained, before his trip to Ohio. Rev. Babcock's father's estate continued to yield him an annual remittance and he preached the word with acceptance. His life was cut short by consumption, but he died in the triumphs of faith,

Henry M. Bacheler
Birth:
Jun. 16, 1849,
India
Death:
Unknown
Burial:
New Hampton Village Cemetery,
New Hampton, Belknap County,
New Hampshire,
Plot: #219

Henry M. Bacheler, M.D., was the son of Rev. Dr. Otis Robinson Bacheler and wife Sarah P. (Merrill) Bacheler. He was born in Balasore, India where his parents were medical and ministerial missionaries. He entered work in India at the close of 1886.

Otis Robinson Batchelder
Birth:
Jan. 17, 1817
Andover, Merrimack County,
New Hampshire
Death:

Jan. 1, 1901
New Hampton,
Belknap County,
New Hampshire
Burial:
New Hampton Village Cemetery,
New Hampton,
Belknap County,
New Hampshire,
Plot: Lot 219

In preparation to become a missionary he studied at Holliston & Wilbraham, MA and Kent's Hill, ME academies, 1835-1839. He studied medicine at Dartmouth & Cambridge Medical colleges. He was licensed to preach by the Boston Quarterly Meeting, Lowell, MA, April 1839 and was ordained an evangelist in Lowell, May 7, 1840.He received his M D from Dartmouth College, 1850; and DD, Hillsdale College, 1881. He sailed for India, May 16,1840 where he was a missionary at Balasore, Orissa, India, October 1840-52; Midnapore, Bengal, 1865-83. Otis returned to the United States, September 1883 and was without charge in New Hampton, 1883-6. Again he sailed from Boston for India, January 23, 1886. He published "A Medical Guide in Oriya and Bengalee." The funeral services for Otis were held in the Free Baptist Church at New Hampton, with the Reverend Atwood B Meservey, DD, PhD, the venerable ex-principal of the New Hampton Literary institution, was to have preached the sermon, but was prevented by sickness, consequently his address was read by Reverend Professor Shirley J Case, of the institution. Others taking part in the services were the Reverend J Burnham Davis, late of Ocean Park, Maine, the Reverend Arthur Given, DD, of Providence, Reverend Robert Ford, of Campton, and Reverend George L White of New Hampton.

Benaiah Bean
Birth:
Jun. 30, 1793
Salisbury,
Merrimack County,
New Hampshire
Death:
Dec. 17, 1856 Colebrook, Coos County,
New Hampshire
Burial:
North Road Cemetery,
Wilmot,
Merrimack County,
New Hampshire

He was converted under the preaching of John Colby and baptized in Feb. 1812, by Rev. Joshua Quimby. He moved to Whitefield in 1821 and became a member of the Freewill Baptist church in that place at its organization. In 1823, he was licensed to preach by the Sandwich Quarterly Meeting. He was ordained August 24, 1828, at Whitefield, where he was pastor for about ten years, witnessing several revivals. At one time he baptized forty-one, at another forty. During the revival which began July 1, 1832, ninety were hopefully converted. While in Whitefield, he labored in Concord, VT, Jefferson and Bethlehem, NH. In 1838 he moved to Bethlehem and was pastor of the church there for eight years. In 1850 he organized the Clarksville and Pittsburg church of fifteen members and became their pastor. Four years later the church numbered sixty. In 1855, the history of Colebrook give the account that Rev. Benaiah Bean organized a Freewill Baptist Church at Colebrook. A church about this time was also organized at Stewartstown, of which he was pastor till his death.

Rev Silas F. Bean
Birth:
Oct. 3, 1807
Death:
Mar. 6, 1890
Burial:
Bean Burial Ground

Tuftonboro
Carroll County
New Hampshire

Ordained Freewill Bapt. minister Dec. 28, 1834. He pastored several churches and until about 80 yrs of age, he preached regularly.
Pastor of First Freewill Baptist Church in Melvin Village from 1839-1866

Rev Hugh Beede
Birth:
Dec. 9, 1807
Sandwich
Carroll County, New Hampshire
Death:
Jan. 27, 1879
Sandwich
Carroll County, New Hampshire
Burial:
Skinners Corners
North Sandwich
Carroll County, New Hampshire

An early NH Freewill Baptist minister; featured in Carroll Co. NH History, and being pastor there.

Lewis P Bickford
Birth:
Oct. 4, 1844
Center Harbor,
Belknap County, New Hampshire
Death:
Aug. 3, 1917
New Hampton,
Belknap County, New Hampshire
Burial:
New Hampton Village Cemetery,
New Hampton,
Belknap County, New Hampshire

He experienced the new birth in 1857 and received license in 1868. He graduated from the New Hampton Institution In 1869 [later Cobb Divinity School, then Bates College]. He received ordination June 31, 1871.

Israel Blake
Birth:
1765
Death:
May 1, 1839
Grafton County,
New Hampshire
Burial:
Blake Cemetery
Stinson Lake
Grafton County,
New Hampshire

He was ordained in the Sandwich Quarterly Meeting in 1800. Here he continued to reside for 40 years. The year 1811 was one of marked revival for his church and quarterly meeting. In 1824 David marks visited him, and in the month of protracted meetings that followed, the church was revived and enlarged. In 1833, 27 members were added by baptism. On May 1, 1839, Brother Blake closed a long service for the master. The Rev. Thomas Perkins preached his funeral sermon from First Thessalonians 4:14.

Simeon Bolles

Birth:
April 16, 1830
Death:
Nov. 18, 1889
Burial:
Maple Street Cemetery
Bethlehem
Grafton County, New Hampshire

He studied at New Hampton Institution and was ordained in Concord, Vt. In 1866 where most of his ministry was. He wrote the History of Bethlehem in 1883.

Rev Hezekiah H Brock

Birth:
1819
Barrington
Strafford County, New Hampshire
Death:
Dec. 30, 1851
Dover
Strafford County, New Hampshire
Burial:
Pine Hill Cemetery
Dover
Strafford County, New Hampshire

Rev. Hezekiah H. Brock was born in Barrington, NH, and embraced the Saviour while young. He was baptized by Eld. Sherburne, and making Dover his residence, he united with the First Free Baptist church there. A year or two afterward, he preached his first sermon.

He did good work at Raymond and afterwards in Kennebunk, ME, where he was ordained in 1845. The next year, he entered the Bible School at Whitestown, NY. His lungs soon after began to fail, and being persuaded that he should not be able to preach further, he turned his attention to medicine.

His young wife died after a year of married life. In Utica, NY, later he married again. In failing health, he removed to Dover, N.H., where he sank rapidly. His last words were "Beautiful Jesus." He died Dec. 30, 1851, aged 31 years. He was amiable in spirit and winning as a preacher.

Rev Joseph Boody
Birth:
May 16, 1752
Barrington
Strafford County
New Hampshire
Death: Jan. 17, 1824
Strafford
Strafford County
New Hampshire
Burial:
Joseph Boody Burial Ground
Strafford
Strafford County
New Hampshire

Son of Azariah Boody (1720-1803) and Bridget (Bushbie) Boody (1720-1785). Children:
John S Boody (1795 - 1874)* One of the converts of the revival that swept through his native town under Rev. Benjamin Randall's preaching.

Rev Joseph Boodey, Jr
Birth:
Apr. 12, 1773
New Hampshire
Death:
May 12, 1867
New Hampshire

Burial:
Old Boodey Place
New Durham
Strafford County
New Hampshire
He was aged 94 yrs. and 1 mo. He was the nephew of another Rev. Joseph Boodey or (Boody) bn 1752, who was shown as companion of Rev. Benj. Randall, whose house was where Eld. Randall and his group of Free Will Baptists organized their church by that name in New Durham.

Free Bapt. Cyclopedia, pub. 1889, records that this Eld. Joseph Boody was the first to preach free salvation in northern Vermont. He had good success but for six months he saw not a minister who gave him a word of cheer.

He was ordained Oct. 18, 1798, at a session of the QM in the New Durham Schoolhouse, with Eld. Benj. Randall, delivering the sermon and Eld. Daniel Lord giving the prayer. He helped organize Quarterly Meetings from the churches that had been organized. He was a worthy minister.

Nahum Brooks
Birth:
Jun. 11, 1811
East Wakefield,
New Hampshire
Death:
Mar. 17, 1883
Manchester,
New Hampshire
Burial:
Valley Cemetery,
Manchester,
Hillsborough County,
New Hampshire,
Plot: 973-3

He was baptized in Aug. 1834 by Rev Samuel Burbank, and joined the church in Wakefield. He acquired a thorough academic education at North Parsonfield under the instruction of the Rev. Hosea Quinby, D.D. He afterward went to Dover, New Hampshire, and was employed in the "Morning Star" office. He began preaching in 1837. Through his efforts a church was organized at Laconia, NH, March 17, 1838, which began with 9 members. He was ordained the following May in 1838 in a session of the Q.M. During this pastorate of six years, he baptized 166 persons. A fine house of worship was built and dedicated Jan 6th, 1841. His next pastorate was at Great Falls, where he baptized 192 converts. In all his pastorates he baptized 653 persons before he contracted a severe cold in a meeting in Candia, which caused partial paralysis of the vocal cords, and in consequence, he was obliged to cease preaching. After his ordination, he attended every session of the NH Yearly Meeting, except four. He was deeply interested in the benevolent enterprises of the denomination and contributed generously to their support. For twenty years, he was an active member of the Foreign Mission Board and two years treasurer of the society. He was also one of the founders of the Maine State Seminary at Lewiston, ME (now Bates)

During his labors there, 160 were added to the church. He also labored successfully in Nashua, Orange, Center Harbor, New Hampton, Hill, and Bridgewater.

He represented Bristol in the legislature of 1847 and 1848. In May 1867, he accepted a call to the pastorate of the Free Baptist Church at Eaton, where a revival of religion was very general.

Amos Brown
Birth:
Sep. 4, 1800
Bristol, Grafton County,
New Hampshire
Death:
Dec. 7, 1867
Eaton Center, Carroll County,
New Hampshire
Burial:
Homeland Cemetery,
Bristol, Grafton County,
New Hampshire,
Plot: Sec. 11E, Lot 3, Grave 7

Amos Brown was licensed to preach by the Sandwich Quarterly Meeting, of the Free Baptist denomination 16 Dec 1829, and was ordained at Alexandria, Grafton, New Hampshire, 30 Sep 1832, by council of elders of the Sandwich Quarterly Meeting, composed of Rev. John Hill, of Alexandria, Rev. Simeon Dana, MD, Rev. Thomas Perkins, of New Hampton, and Rev. Devi Smith. He labored one-half the time at Alexandria from 1837 till 1853, and had pastoral oversight of the church for thirty-seven years.

William Burr
Birth:
Jun. 22, 1806
Hingham Center,
Plymouth County,
Massachusetts
Death:
Nov. 5, 1866
Dover, Strafford County,
New Hampshire
Burial::
Pine Hill Cemetery,
Dover, Strafford County,
New Hampshire

While in his early teens, he apprenticed with a Boston printer, learning the trade he would put to good use for the Free Will Baptist Printing Establishment. Their books included his name among those they hold in high esteem.

A biography, *Life of William Burr*, was written in 1871 by Rev. J. M. Brewster.

An inscription on the 12-ft marble monument erected over his grave reads: WILLIAM BURR, age 60. This Monument, erected by the Freewill Baptist Denomination stands as a tribute to his memory. He had charge of the Printing Office at the opening in 1826, and was Editor of the *Morning Star* and Agent of the Printing Establishment during a period of more than thirty years. By his integrity in business, his urbanity in social intercourse,

His broad and philanthropic sympathies, especially by his devout earnestness and as a Christian, he won and retained the high esteem of all who knew him.

He was a member of the City Government in Dover, the Legislature of New Hampshire; and for twenty-five consecutive years was elected Treasurer of the Benevolent Societies. He was a strong abolitionist and at a anti-slavery meeting sat beside President Abraham Lincoln.

Elder Hezekiah D Buzzell
Birth:
Dec. 16, 1777
Alton,
Belknap County, New Hampshire
Death:
Sep. 6, 1858
Alton, Belknap County,
New Hampshire
Burial:
Hurd Cemetery, Alton,
Belknap County,
New Hampshire

Buzzell was ordained in Gilmanton, New Hampshire on Jan 25, 1803, then preached in Alton, Gilmanton and Weare for fifty years. He was a minister at the Free Will Baptist Church in Weare (established October 20, 1806) from March 8, 1812 to 1829. He served as a State Rep in the New Hampshire House of Representatives from 1814 to 1816 and again 1819-1820, and as a State Senator in the New Hampshire 3rd District 1822-1823.

Aaron Buzzell
Birth:
Dec. 31, 1764
Gilmanton,
Belknap County, New Hampshire
Death:
Oct. 21, 1854
Barrington, Strafford County,
New Hampshire
Burial:
Pine Grove Cemetery,
Barrington, Strafford County,
New Hampshire

Rev. Aaron and his brother Rev. John Buzzell and Rev. Benjamin Randall were the people who started the Free Will Baptist Church of Middleton in 1790. The branches of both brothers and family members were all Free Will Baptists.

Alvah Buzzell
Birth:
Apr. 12, 1807
Parsonsfield,
York County, Maine
Death:
Apr. 2, 1888 Southborough,
Worcester County,
Massachusetts
Burial:
Lake View Cemetery,
East Andover,
Merrimack County,
New Hampshire

Reverend Alvah Buzzell, son of Reverend John Buzzell, was born in Parsonfield, Maine on April 11, 1807. He was converted at the age of eighteen and ordained as pastor of the church at Barnstead, New Hampshire in June 1834 by Reverend Enoch Place. He has had the care of twelve churches and helped organized six churches. He has baptized many hundreds. At the breaking out of the Civil War, when he was fifty-four, he followed his sons Frank and John to the front, caring for the sick and wounded, and preaching the gospel and helping the Negro to school privileges.

David Calley
Birth:
Nov. 8, 1815
Holderness, Grafton County
New Hampshire
Death:
Dec. 23, 1906
Bristol, Grafton County
New Hampshire,
Burial:
Green Grove Cemetery
Ashland, Grafton County
New Hampshire

David Calley's career as a clergyman was a remarkable one. At the age of 23 years he professed religion, and the next year, 1837, he received a license to preach. In May 1942, at a session of the Sandwich Quarterly Meeting he was ordained, and a month later became the pastor of the Free Baptist Church at North Tunbridge, Vermont, where he remained until 1847. In September 1852 he began his second pastorate at Bristol, which continued for seven years. He then returned to Tunbridge, Vermont. Where he remained three years, and again assumed the pastoral charge of the church at Bristol and continued for another seven years. He thus served the Bristol church as pastor for sixteen years. To no other man does the Free Baptist Church of Bristol owe so much as to the Reverend David Calley. He was a man of great natural ability, an excellent preacher, devoted, godly and his pure life and labors endeared him to all classes in the community. He was of fine personal presence, standing six feet two inches. Mr Calley four times had a seat in the Legislature. He represented Holderness in 1853, Bristol in 1872, and 1873 and Sandwich in 1885.

Carter E Cate
Birth:
Aug. 26, 1852
Loudon
Merrimack County
New Hampshire
Death:
Jan. 18, 1927
Cranston
Providence County
Rhode Island

Burial:
Bayside Cemetery
Laconia
Belknap County, New Hampshire

He graduated at Dartmouth College in 1876 and studied for the ministry at Boston University. His ministry was in the states of New Hampshire, Vermont, Mass., Maine and Rhode Island. His last pastorate was with the Roger Williams Church in Providence, Rhode Island 1897-1895. Spouse: Electa A. Dunavan Cate (1854 - 1929).

John Caverly
Birth:
Aug. 23, 1789
Barrington
Strafford County
New Hampshire
Death:
Mar. 23, 1863
Strafford
Strafford County
New Hampshire
Burial:
Caverly Hill Cemetery

Strafford
Strafford County
New Hampshire

Rev. John Caverly died of heart disease in his 74th year. He was the eldest son of Lieutenant John Caverly and his mother was a sister of Rev. Joseph Boody, all of Strafford. He was converted in the famous revival of 1824, and June 2nd was baptized and joined the Third Strafford church. About a later he began to preach and at the request from his church a council from the New Durham Quarterly Meeting (QM) met at his church and ordained him Sept. 6, 1827, as an evangelist in the presence of 1000 persons. He soon entered upon a life-long pastorate with the Fourth Strafford church. He had a revival gift. He loved his denomination and was true to her benevolent interests. He was trustee of Strafford Academy nearly twenty years at an expense to himself of over $300 besides his time. He was an agent for a large manufacturing company for many years, bearing large and responsible interests. The house of worship at Bow Lake was erected by his means and influence. His wife, Miss Nancy French of New Durham, died in 1855 leaving four children. For several years he bore up with patience and trust under the disease which caused his death. He selected Rev. Enoch Place to preach his funeral sermon.

Arthur Caverno
Birth:
Apr. 6, 1801
Strafford, Strafford County,
New Hampshire
Death:
Jul. 15, 1876
Dover, Strafford County,
New Hampshire
Burial:
Pine Hill Cemetery,
Dover, Strafford County,
New Hampshire

Caverno died at aged 75 years.

He was the son of Jeremiah and Mary Brewster Caverno, and great-grandson of Arthur Caverno (or Cavano), of Scotch Irish nationality, who came to this country soon after 1735.

He was born in Strafford (then Barrington), N. H., He was in a twofold sense one of the fathers of the denomination. He had been more than fifty-four years in its ministry, and, at a formative period of its history, he exerted a controlling influence.

When seventeen years of age he became a Christian, after a severe struggle with unbelief occasioned by deep conviction of sin. He was baptized by Rev. Enoch Place, Oct. 11, 1818. He attended Gilmanton Academy six months, and afterwards studied in th academy at Newfield's village in New Market. He obtained what was, in those days, an excellent academic education and taught school successfully in various places. He yielded more cheerfully than many to the call to preach, and began at the age of nineteen. Aug. 23, 1822, at the age of twenty-one he was licensed by the New Durham Q. M. He was ordained June 17, 1823, in an oak grove on his father's homestead by a council consisting of Rev's Samuel B. Dyer, Moses Bean, David Harriman, Enoch Place and William Buzzell. David Harriman preached the sermon.

He was married December 23d to Mrs. Olive H. Foss of Strafford.

The next year he taught school in Epsom.

Through his ministry there a church was gathered of which he was pastor till the autumn of 1827. The revival, the first year, was extensive. He also preached and baptized in Nottingham and Raymond. Rev. D. P. Cilley and two other ministers were converted ouring this time.

His second pastorate was at Contoocook. His first sermon there was published in the *Morning Star*. Text, "The Powers Of Heaven Shall Be Shaken."

The first year, 1830, a revival of remarkable power and extent was witnessed. People were converted at their homes, in their shops, on their farms, going to and returning from meetings. The church more than doubled its membership and the good influence of the work lasted many years. He continued there five years. For three years, ending in 1836, he was pastor at Great Falls; the next two years financial agent of Strafford Academy; pastor of Roger Williams church, Providence, R. I. one year, eliding in the fall of 1839; assistant pastor in Lowell, Mass., six months; pastor in Charleston, Mass., two and a half years; pastor in Bangor, Me., three years, ending in the fall of 1845; stated supply in Portsmouth, N. H., at the Old South, until the spring of 1847; pastor in Candia two years; pastor in Dover three years, when the house of worship was changed to its present locality on Charles Street; stated supply in Concord several months in 1852, and several months in South Berwick, Me.; then pastor two years in Biddeford, Me.

His wife, who had helped him thirty-one years, died in Dover, N. H., Jan. 30, J854.

The next year he married Mrs. Isabel J. Sule, of Bath, Me.

He preached for the First church, Dover, a year, then in New Market a year. For two years, ending in 1860, he was pastor in Gardiner, Me. He then preached in Strafford Centre, Laconia, and Alton Corner, a few months in each place. For two years, ending in 1866, he was pastor at South Parsonfield, Me.

He next lived in Great Falls, N. H., and preached for the Baptist church at Little River Falls in Lebanon, Me., and in Berwick at Cranberry Meadow. Then he was pastor in North Berwick two years, and lastly in Candia again two years. In some places there were revivals, in others he trained the forces.

He was a preacher fifty-six years, an ordained minister fifty-three years. He preached 6,000 sermons, baptized 480 persons, married 320 couples, and attended 500 funerals. As a preacher, he was systematic in his presentation of truth, apt and forcible in his illustrations. He was a diligent student of the Bible and a careful observer' of men and things about him. His usual method was to preach from a well-prepared skeleton, and many of his sermons were afterwards 'written out in full. He possessed a voice of more than ordinary sweetness and power.

He was affable and courteous in manner, social in disposition, and a general favorite in all the families where he was known.

He helped forward every denominational enterprise.

He began to write for the *Morning Star* the first year of its existence, and contributed more or less every year during his life. His last article appeared in the number issued during the week of his death. He early published a series on the "Support of the Ministry," which helped to introduce the practice of stipulated salaries. He was himself the first minister in the denomination who received a stipulated. Salary.

He had great influence in removing the practice of feet washing which prevailed in some measure.

He was a member of the first General Conference, and assisted in organizing the Home and Foreign Mission Societies. He was greatly interested in all the educational movements. Other good causes received his earnest support. He lectured often in many places on temperance, and helped in the organization of some of the earliest Total Abstinence Societies in New Hampshire. He labored much for the abolition of capital punishment.

His last years were spent in Dover. The Sunday before his death he preached in Alton. His funeral services were conducted by Rev. Joseph Fullonton one of his early converts.

Rev Daniel Plummer Cilley
Birth:
May 31, 1806
Manchester, Hillsborough,
New Hampshire
Death:
Nov. 14, 1888
Burial:
Pine Grove Cemetery

Farmington
Strafford County
New Hampshire

U.S., Civil War Soldier Records and Profiles, 1861-1865 commissioned an officer in Company S, New Hampshire 8th Infantry Regiment on 28 Dec 1861. Mustered out on 17 Jan 1865.

A leading Free Will Baptist minister in the Northeastern movement

Peter Clark
Birth:
October 8, 1781
Upper Gilmanton, New Hampshire
Death:
November 25, 1865
Upper Gilmanton, New Hampshire
Burial:
Highland Cemetery
Belmont
Belknap County,
New Hampshire, Plot: D

He was born in Dialogue and had the example and instruction of a faithful mother who early told him the value of prayer. He was converted in June 1798 and was baptized by Elder R. Martin. In the next September he began his ministry in his native place. Elder Martin pointed them out to a bystander as a boy was hard to handle it in argument. In January 8, 1810 he was ordained by the Rev.'s Winthrop Young, R. Martin, and Hezekiah D. Buzzell. He became the pastor of the newly organized Third Gilmanton church. Great revivals followed and there were added on April 20, 24; August 22, eight; June 25, 1814, 22; October, 18, 31. In 1826 this independent church joined the New Durham Quarterly Meeting. In the 1829 session of the quarterly meeting a revival commenced which continued for months, spreading elsewhere, and in November there were 18 added to the church in others through the winter. A healthy growth existed in the church for years. And in its early days beginning in about 1830 the church began to have great interest in the cause of temperance. He represented his town in the legislature and was given to Christian hospitality.

Inscription:
Died in his 63rd yrs of Ministry.

Rev Stephen Coffin
Birth:
Mar. 8, 1792
Alton, Belknap County
New Hampshire
Death:
Mar. 4, 1867

Dover, Strafford County
New Hampshire
Burial:
Pine Hill Cemetery
Dover, Strafford County
New Hampshire
Plot: Sec 5 - Ave M

Ordained a Freewill Baptist minister in 1841, and was useful to the cause he loved, giving liberally of his means to its benevolent enterprises. His Daughter Christiana Cowell was an author and the wife of Rev. David Cowell.

Clefford Cole, Sr
Birth:
Jun. 11, 1772
Massachusetts
Death:
Sep. 15, 1852
Stark
Coos County
New Hampshire
Burial:
Percy Cemetery
Stark
Coos County
New Hampshire

Clefford was the son of Jonathon and Elizabeth [Crowning shield] Cole. His step-brother, John, was the very first man to settle in Percy. Clefford followed shortly after and built a log cabin. Their elderly father joined them later in 1791.

He married Janet "Jint" Rowell, daughter of Capt. Daniel Rowell and Judith French. He was a farmer and a Free Will Baptist minister. They had eleven children

Inscription:
CLEFFORD COLE
June 11, 1772
Sept. 15, 1852

Rev Clefford Cole, Jr
Birth:
Feb. 16, 1813
Percy
Coos County, New Hampshire
Death:
Jun. 10, 1882
Stark
Coos County
New Hampshire
Burial:
Percy Cemetery
Stark, Coos County
New Hampshire

Clefford is the son of Clefford Cole and Janet Rowell, daughter of Capt. Daniel Rowell. His father and uncle were the very first men to settle in Percy.

He was a shoemaker, station agent, Free Will Baptist preacher, and Fort Master. Licensed to preach 1842; 25-30 added to church first year. Ordained Jan 13, 1845, became pastor of Milan & Stark Church.

On Sept 25, 1834 in Stark he married Almira Leavitt, daughter of Peter Leavitt Jr. and Mehitable Marden.

Inscription:
CLEFFORD COLE
DIED
June 10, 1882
AE. 69ys. 3ms.
& 22ds.

"He died rejoicing in that Jesus,
He had loved and labored for so long
Saying in his last hours,
It is blessed dying with Jesus."

Samuel Cole
Birth:
Unknown
Salem, New Hampshire
Death:
Mar. 7, 1850
Lisbon, New Hampshire
Burial:
Sunny Side Cemetery
Grafton County, New Hampshire

In 1798 he moved to Landaff where at the age of 21 was converted. After deep conviction, he began to hold meetings and was ordained in 1827. His labors as a minister were confined mostly to Lisbon and Landaff. He supported a large family by diligence and yet found time to engage much in the labor for his master.

Solomon Cole
Birth:
July 8, 1821
Whitefield, New Hampshire
Death:
1902
New Hampshire
Burial:
Glenwood Cemetery
Lebanon
Grafton County, New Hampshire
Plot: sec a; Lot O

In a session of the New Hampshire Yearly Meeting about 1836, he was converted under the preaching of David marks and four years later was baptized by the Rev. Beniah Bean of Whitefield. At that time he felt called to the ministry, but put off the work for 20 years because of his lack of preparation. However, during this time he began holding meetings in needy places. He received license to preach about 1870 and was ordained in 1876 by Rev. C. N. Nelson and others. His early ministry enjoyed revivals and saw hundreds come to the Lord. He was a member of the firm of S. Cole and Sons Iron Founders and Machinists, Lebanon, New Hampshire, so he was able to preach the gospel to the needy without compensation. In 1846 he married Miss Caroline F. Peasley. He also served four terms in the New Hampshire legislature.

Charles Corson
Birth:
1788
Lebanon, Maine
Death:
1860
New Hampshire
Burial:
Rochester Cemetery
Rochester
Strafford County,
New Hampshire

He was converted about 1820 and was baptized by Rev. David Blaisdell joining the Free Baptist Church in Lebanon. He began preaching soon after. After preaching several years he was ordained about 1840 and was associated with Rev. Blaisdell and Cupp. He was not a revival preacher, but was instructive. His words were mighty through the excellent character of the man behind them.

Christ Has Led the Way

Thomas Cotton
Birth:
Nov. 16, 1766
Death:
Aug. 5, 1847
Wolfborough,
NH
Burial:
Cotton Mountain Cemetery
Wolfeboro
Carroll County,
New Hampshire

He was a farmer, deacon, and occasional preacher, "a man of very fervid religious Character."
Family: Spouse: Martha Cotton (1768 - 1857), Children: Daniel Cotton (1803 - 1865), Saloma Cotton (1808 - 1823).

Arthur Elmes Cox
Birth:
May 25, 1858
Princes Risborough,
Buckinghamshire, England
Death:
May 21, 1942
New Hampshire
Burial:

New Hampton Village Cemetery
New Hampton
Belknap County New Hampshire,
Plot: #182

Rev. Cox immigrated to the U.S. in 1872. He married Elizabeth Anna Hayes, daughter of Prof. Benjamin F. Hayes, of Lewiston, ME. Cox studied at Richmond College, Virginia, and theology at Cobb Divinity School. He was converted in 1869, and was ordained to the ministry June 24, 1883, by Rev's J.J. Hall, C.E. Cate, J. Fullerton, B.F. Hayes, and J.S. Burgess. He was a Freewill Baptist minister and held pastorates at Garner, W. Pike, Pennsylvania; Little Falls and Windham Center, Maine.

Jesse Cross
Birth:
June 9, 1790
Newbury,
New Hampshire
Death:
November 1, 1865
New Hampshire
Burial:
Church Place Cemetery
Wilmot
Merrimack County,
New Hampshire

In his early years he committed to memory, through the example in inspiration of the pious mother a large portion of the Bible. He acquired the rudiments of education in the common schools and when he was about 20 he was converted under the preaching of Rev. Timothy Morse and 10 years later was licensed by Weare Quarterly Meeting meeting. In 1840 he was ordained by the same body as pastor of the Springfield church, of which he had been many years a member. For 40 years he labored among the churches in Sullivan and Merrimack County and witnessed a precious outpourings of the spirit of God. His sermons were highly biblical, ernest and pathetic; his prayers were tender and suppository, yet wonderfully full of faith and power. He preached much in secret. He was a member of the Second Wilmot Church at the time of his death.

Silas Curtis
Birth:
Feb. 27, 1804
Minot,
Androscoggin County, Maine

Death:
Jan. 27, 1893
Concord,
Merrimack County,
New Hampshire
Burial:
Blossom Hill Cemetery,
Concord, Merrimack County,
New Hampshire

In the schools of Lewiston and Greene he laid the foundation of his education. He prepared for College in the Maine Wesleyan Seminary at Kent's Hill, but had health problems and could not continue. He was converted at age 17 was baptized by Rev. B. Thorn, and joined the Free Will Baptist church at Lewiston in May 1821. After his 21st year, he taught school several winters in Lewiston and Lisbon. In the spring of 1827, at age 23, he began to preach the gospel. He was ordained Oct. 4, 1827, when Bowdoin Q.M was in session at Topsham, Maine. Ordaining members were Rev's Geo. Lamb, Aliezer Bridges, and Allen Files. He travelled and preached all around the area for the next three or four years. He pastored in Lynn, Mass, but the ocean air did not agree with his health, and thus, he became pastor of the Lowell church for five years. In Lowell. From 1852-1856, he pastored in Pittsfield, NH, and from there to Concord, NH, where he pastored. During his ministry he baptized 800 converts, assisted in organizing several churches and preached at the dedication of twelve church edifices. he was active and influential in every denominational enterprise.

He was foremost in the era of publication and educational institutions and organization of benevolent societies. In 1832, he was selected as one of the printing committee of the Printing Establishment and continued on that board for over 40 years, and was interim agent after William Burr's death.

He was appointed agent, and raised $17,000 for the New Hampton Institution, and gathered funds for Chapel Hall. He was corresponding Secretary of the Home Mission Society from 1839-1869, when he resigned. Also, he served on the Foreign Mission Society. In 1865, he spent several weeks in South Carolina and Virginia, superintendent of the work among the freedmen, and afterwards visited the schools and mission stations in Shenandoah Valley, and Storer College at Harper's Ferry. He was clerk of the General Conference in 1835 until 1868. He attended 20 of the 26 General Conferences. He made his home in Concord, New Hampshire for more than 30 years. In Concord, he was an esteemed member and Vice-President, of the "New Hampshire Bible Society" until his death. They recorded in their 1893 minutes at his death, "Rev. Silas Curtis, D.D., was removed by death"

Jacob Burnham Davis
Birth:
Oct. 6, 1830
Nottingham
Rockingham County
New Hampshire
Death:
May 29, 1905
New Hampshire Burial:
Homeland Cemetery
Bristol
Grafton County
New Hampshire
Plot: Sec. 16E, Lot 8, Grave 7

He was the son of Jacob and Anna (Davis) Davis and the husband of Mary Ann Perkins. They married on May 28, 1861
He studied at New Hampton Institution and graduated from its Theological School, 1859. He also attended Andover Theological Seminary May 1861-5. He was Ordained in Lawrence, Mass., June 21, 1861. He pastored in Mass., Rhode Island, Maine and Illinois.

He baptized over 400; solemnized 228 marriages; and officiated at more than 800 funerals.

Note: Additional information from *Native Ministry of New Hampshire.*

John Davis
Birth:
Sept. 1, 1802
Death:
Nov. 10, 1885
South Boston, Mass.
Burial:
Elkins Cemetery
Belmont, Belknap County,
New Hampshire
Plot: 10

Ordained 1830 at Bethlehem, and pastor 1830-8; the moved to Vermont where he ministered a number of churches until 1880 when he moved to Mass. And pastored two churches departing this life at South Boston while pastor.

Inscription:
I have fought a good fight, I have kept faith.

Robert Dickey
Birth:
Jun. 11, 1764
Boston
Suffolk County, Massachusetts
Death:
Jan. 2, 1849
Burial:
Bunker Hill Cemetery
Wilmot
Merrimack County,
New Hampshire

He was a member of Benjamin Randall's church and at New Durham, New Hampshire and went from Epsom, N.H. to Work as a laborer with a relative in Stafford, Vermont. The young man was touched by the spiritual needs of the place and began his preaching and witnessed over 30 converted. On September 10, 1791 a letter was addressed to the New Durham church desiring church orders. Benjamin Randall and John Buzzell and several times visited these brothers. It was the first Free Will Baptist church in Vermont to be organized in the spring of 1793. In june 1794 Robert Dickey was a delegate of this church with a letter to the New Hampshire Yearly Meeting for membership. He subsequently became a useful minister being ordained in 1814, but later his usefulness was lost when he joined the Shakers.

Because He Rose, We Too Shall Rise.

Samuel B Dyer
Birth:
March 21, 1779
New Market, NH
Death:
Nov. 19, 1846
Deerfield
New Hampshire
Burial:
Loudon Center Cemetery
Merrimack County
New Hampshire

When about three yrs of age his parents removed to Pittsfield where he grew up. He was trained from a child to hard work, which contributed to his possessing one of the best physical constitutions. He stood a little less than six feet, had a fine commanding form, with full, expressive eyes, and black hair, and was a fair-looking young man. He gave himself to God under the preaching of Rev. Aaron Buzzell, was baptized by Rev. Benj. Randall in 1798, and from then on he entered into the work of God.

He was married three times:
1) Mrs. Abigail Fogg, on 5th May, 1801. He set up his trade as a clothier, to support his rising family

and his aging parents, laboring in his mill from 12 to 14 hrs a day.

On March 7, 1804, he was ordained at Nottingham, and subsequently took charge of the FWB church in that town. He was blessed in this ministry.

He soon became extensively known to the public, and highly esteemed as an able minister, so that calls to funerals, marriages, baptisms, and other work, became so frequent he relinquished his clothing business and purchased a farm.

He was elected three times to the State Legislature. He left that place to devote his time to the ministry. He removed to Loudon in 1822, purchased a good farm and was well supported. He gathered a large church. Notwithstanding, the prosperity, he suffered the loss of hiswife, Abigail, Aug. 9, 1825, the wife of his youth, and the mother of twelve children---eleven who were then living.

He bore it with manly fortitude believing she was one of the most pious, amiable, and industrious women, but was in the end, her eternal gain.

2) On Feb. 21, 1826, he married Mrs Jemima Clough, a woman of good Christian character, benevolence of feeling toward his children, and was a good wife to him. But on the 18 of Nov. 1837, Jemima died, having helped raise nearly all his children. He resolved on visiting his children in Ohio, and declined a second term to state office.

3) After his return, he married Mrs. Betsey Morrill, of Gilmanton, the 12 of Dec. 1838. She was a lady possessing respectable accomplishments, and a good estate. In June 1839, they removed from Loudon to Deerfield, where God blessed his labors.

He was an ordained minister more than forty-two years, in which time he baptized many hundreds, solemnized between 700-1000 marriages and preached nearly 2,000 funeral sermons. He took great interest in the Deerfield/Nottingham QM, and attended for the last time in 1846, prayed at the ordination of two young ministers, which so affected many that it caused them to remark that they "would never hear Mr. Dyer pray again."

He represented Nottingham in the Legislature, 1817-8. And was a State Senator, 1888..

He died from typhus fever which ended in quick consumption. Rev. Enoch Place preached his funeral, and the procession then went 18 miles to Loudon to lay him beside two of his wives.

Info taken from "Eminent Preachers" by Selah H. Barrett, printed in 1874.

Son of Samuel B. Dyer & Abigail Fogg; Samuel B. Dyer, died Feb. 9, 1897 in Hillsdale, Michigan. The source for this is found on Familysearch.org in Michigan Deaths, 1867-1897. The memorial for Samuel B. Dyer Jr. shows his parents as Samuel Dyer, this Samuel Dyer was married to Lucretia Evans, they did have a son named Samuel who died at the age of 2 years.

Inscription:
Elder Samuel B. Dyer
Died Nov. 19, 1846 AE 67 ys 8
Ms.Abigail His Wife
Died Aug. 9, 1825 AE 42
Jemima His Wife
Died Nov. 18, 1837 AE 55
Side of stone;
Keziah B.
Died Sept. 17, 1831 AE 21
Edmund E.
Died at sea Feb. 1842 AE 21
Children of
Elder Samuel B. & Abigail Dyer

Andrew J. Eastman
Birth:
Jul. 23, 1846
East Parsonsfield,
York County, Maine
Death:
1918
Burial:
Blair Cemetery,
Campton Lower Village,

Grafton County,
New Hampshire,
Plot: A 85
He graduated from Bates College in 1974 and the Bates Theological School in 1977. He was ordained in the Steep falls, Maine Quarterly Meeting on November 1, 1877 by the Cumberland Quarterly Meeting. He held a number of pastorates in the state of Massachusetts and recorded many baptisms.

Daniel Elkins
Birth:
1760
Lee
Strafford County,New Hampshire
Death:
Jun. 4, 1845
Jackson
Carroll County,New Hampshire
Burial:
Jackson Village Cemetery
Jackson
Carroll County, New Hampshire

He moved to Gilmanton and in 1797. In 1799 he held meetings on Meredith Hill. In 1804 he had a revival in Jackson, and by request of the converts he was ordained at the quarterly meeting held at Sandwich, by Rev. Benjamin Randall and John Buzzell. He immediately returned to Jackson, where he baptized several, formed a church and soon made his home. Here he had a useful ministry for 40 years.

Rev Ebenezer Nichols Fernald

Birth:
Mar. 10, 1833
West Lebanon
York County
Maine
Death:
Jan. 15, 1898
Acton
York County
Maine
Burial:
Joseph Fernald Cemetery
Lebanon
York County
Maine

Rev. Ebenezer N. FERNALD, was the son of Joseph and Polly (Nichols) Fernald. He was converted in 1842. He was fitted for college at New Hampton, NH, from 1855-58. In Aug. 1858, he entered Amherst College (MA) and graduated in 1862. After teaching four years he entered Andover Theological Seminary, and graduated in 1869. He was licensed to preach in 1868, and ordained by

a council of the Boston Quarterly Meeting (QM) in Dec. 1869. He was pastor of a church which he organized at Winthrop, Mass, from 1868 to 1870. From 1870-1874, he was pastor of the church in Auburn, Maine. The next two years he was corresponding secretary of the Education Society. From 1876 to 1883 he was financial secretary of the Home Mission, Foreign Mission, and Education Societies [Freewill Baptist], and treasurer of the same societies until 1885.

He then became publisher of "The Morning Star,". He was married Dec. 27, 1863, to Miss Anna B. Tuxbury. Mrs. Fernald was a member of the board of managers of the Woman's Missionary Society.

Rev Jonathan Fletcher

Birth:
Feb. 22, 1802
Maine
Death: Jan. 17, 1881
New Hampshire
Burial:
Eaton Center Cemetery
Eaton Center
Carroll County
New Hampshire,

Rev. Jonathan Fletcher, received license for the ministry in 1838, and in 1839, he was ordained by the Sandwich Quarterly Meeting (QM).

He was pastor of the Albany church till 1851, of the Third Eaton church the next three years, and of the Second Eaton church till 1871. From that year until his death he was pastor of the First Eaton Church. He preached also in Madison, Conway and Effingham.

He married Thirsa Allard, b. NH, and on 1850 census, they have daughters, Esther, 22, and Betsy, 13, both b. NH.

Timothy Flanders
Birth:
Jan. 12, 1787
Death:
June 17, 1849
Burial:
North Road Cemetery
Wilmot
Merrimack County
New Hampshire

Ordained Wilmot, Sept. 29, 1840. Timothy Flanders 63 yrs. and wife Abigail 77 yrs. Spouse: Nabby Abigail Robie Flanders (1788 - 1866).

Rev Nathaniel K George
Birth:
Apr. 2, 1816
Washington
Orange County, Vermont
Death:
Jun. 19, 1860
Franconia
Grafton County
New Hampshire
Burial:
Elmwood Cemetery
Franconia
Grafton County
New Hampshire

Nathaniel was the son of Joshua and Rhoda GEORGE. He was converted in Jan. 1831, and ws baptized in April by Rev. H.N. Plumb, and united with the Corinth (Freewill Baptist) church, where Rev. N. Bowles was pastor. He began to feel the call to the ministry and delivered his first sermon in a schoolhouse in the town of Bethlehem, in 1835. He travelled during the spring and summer preaching through the northern part of NH and VT, and in Warner, N.H, he spent the winter. He saw many converted and added to the churches as he held meetings at various places.

Nov. 14, 1836, he married Sarah C. Kibbey, dau of Deacon John Kibbey of Lyndon, VT. Census shows he and his wife had two daughters, Sarah and Zillah George.

His first settled pastorate was in Washington, his native town, in May 1838. In 1839, he became pastor of the church at Franconia, NH. During four years of his six years pastorate one hundred were added to the church. He also pastored the Whitefield church, and Springvale, ME, church. Returning to Franconia for a visit, previous to a settlement at Bath, ME, while coming from the field on horseback, June 19, 1860, both himself and horse were killed by lightning. Only a week before he had attended a meeting of the Foreign Mission Board, of which he was a faithful member. He also met in the NH Yearly Meeting for twenty-three times.

Rev. Jonathan Woodman preached his funeral sermon from the text Matt 24:27, while six or eight of his intimate friends in the ministry, bore his remains to their last resting place. He died in his 45th year, twenty-five of which he had spent in the ministry. During this time between five and six hundred had been converted and added to churches. He was an ardent lover of truth, advocating all the benevolent enterprises of the denomination.

Joseph Granville
Birth:
Jan. 6, 1816
Death:
Jun. 8, 1897
Burial:
Village Cemetery
Fremont
Rockingham County
New Hampshire

Ordained by the New Durham QM 1865 and labored in New Hampshire, Maine, Nova Scotia and Vermont. Spouse: Abigail K. Allard Granville (1818 - 1893)

David Garland
Birth:
Dec. 18, 1791
Death:
Feb. 6, 1863
Burial:
Garland Family Cemetery,
Center Barnstead,
Belknap County, New Hampshire

His ministry was confined to the New Hampshire area.

Orison Levi Gile
Birth:
Oct. 22, 1856
Bennington
Hillsborough County
New Hampshire

Death:
May 31, 1892
Bowdoinham
Sagadahoc County
Maine
Burial:
Sunnyside Cemetery
Bennington
Hillsborough County
New Hampshire

Studied at New Hampton Institution. Was a traveling agent for YMCA for a time and graduated from Bates College 1883 and Cobb Divinity School, 1886. His ministry was mainly in Maine. Married to Lina E. Nelson on Jan. 1, 1884 in Richimond, Maine. Born: Sutton, New Hampshire. Died: 25 Jan 1886 in Lewiston, Maine. Married to Sarah Eliza Libby on Jun. 22, 1887 in Richmond, Maine. Born: 13 Aug 1865. Died: 23 Jan 1931 in Bowdoinham, Penobscot, Maine.

Rev Edmund T. Gilman
Birth:
Feb. 21, 1844
Ossipee, NH

Death:
Jul. 7, 1925
Burial:
Gilman Cemetery
Tamworth
Carroll County
New Hampshire

He took the Methodist Local Preachers' course of three years, and was licensed by them at Great Falls, NH, in Feb. 1879. He taught and preached in neglected districts and Ossipee, NH. In 1885-86, he was a colporteur (seller/peddler of religious materials) of the New Hampshire Bible Society in Carroll and Coos Counties. On May 20, 1886, he was baptized by immersion and joined the Free Baptist church at Tamworth Iron Works. He was licensed by the Exeter Q.M. Dec. 11, 1887, ME. and was pastor at No. Guilford, in the same year. In 1888 he was engaged in missionary work in Willimantic, ME.

Moulton Hackett

Birth:
1772
New Hampshire
Death:
Oct. 10, 1830
New Hampton, Belknap County,
New Hampshire
Burial:
Chandler Cemetery,
New Hampton,
Belknap County,NewHampshire,
Plot: Grave 9

New Hampshire FWB Minister.

Ezra Ham

Birth:
Mar. 7, 1797
Farmington, Strafford County,
New Hampshire
Death:
Feb. 16, 1880
Gilmanton,
Belknap County, NewHampshire
Burial: Smith Meeting House
Cemetery,
Gilmanton,
Belknap County, NewHampshire

He became a Christian in early life, but did not enter the ministry till forty-three years of age. He was ordained a Freewill Baptist minister at Gilmanton Iron Works, New Hampshire, in 1840. He was instrumental in the organization of the church there and it was largely through his efforts that the meeting house was built. He was pastor of the church several years. In 1867-68, he represented his town in the Legislature; the latter term he served as chaplain of the House.

Moses Hanson
Birth:
Aug., 1792
Ossipee
Carroll County, New Hampshire
Death:
Nov. 21, 1868
Wolfeboro
Carroll County, New Hampshire
Burial:
Ossipee Town Cemetery
Ossipee, Carroll County,
New Hampshire

His father died when he was seven, and he was put out in a good home till he, reached his majority. In the war of 1812,as a musician, he served his country several months at Portsmouth. He married Oct. 1, 1815, Miss Joanna Hansom. At the death of his second child, in 1821, he was seriously convicted, but he did not yield his heart till the winter of 1829,and in 1830 was baptized by Rev. John Pinkham, joining the Second Ossipee church. The next year he was chosen deacon, and served the church well till he was dismissed with others to form the Fourth Ossipee church. He was licensed in 1838, and ordained in 1840. In June, 1842, his wife died; in 1843 he married Miss Hannah Seavey, who survived him. He preached in Effingham, N. H., and in Porter, Me., and finally came to Wolfborough, where he finished his course. He was earnest in reform and eminently a man of prayer.

Inscription:
"With heavenly weapons I have fought The battles of the Lord. Finished my course, and kept the faith, And wait the sure reward."

Pelatiah Hanscom
Birth:
1796
Kittery, Maine
Death:
Apr. 20, 1857
Epping, New York
Burial:
South Hampton Cemetery
South Hampton
Rockingham County,
New Hampshire

Early in his life he went to Barnstead, where he was converted and baptized by the Rev. n. Wilson. Receiving a license to preach, he moved to Lyman, Maine where he enjoyed a good revival. In 1837, he moved to Exeter, New Hampshire and connected himself with the Stratham church and did a good work in that locality. On July 5, 1839, he was ordained by a Council consisting of the

Reverends John Kimball. S. P. Fernald, E. True, and J. Fullonton. He soon had the satisfaction of baptizing his wife and his only daughter. After moving to Epping, he organized a church there in 1840.

Joseph Morrill Harper

Birth:
Jun. 21, 1787
Limerick
York County, Maine
Death:
Jan. 15, 1865
Canterbury, Merrimack County,
New Hampshire
Burial:
Canterbury Village Cemetery
Canterbury, Merrimack County,
New Hampshire

He attended Fryeburg Academy, studied medicine, and in 1810 began a practice in Sanbornton, New Hampshire, later moving to Canterbury, where he was a physician for 30 years. Converted in October 1810 he was baptized uniting with the church in Canterbury. He was ordained on April 11, 1838 and preached for more than 27 years. He was the moderator of the Ninth General Conference at Greenville, Rhode Island in October 2018; of the 10th at Conneaut, Ohio in October 1837; of the 11th, at Topsham, Maine, in October 1841. Harper was a veteran of the War of 1812, serving as Assistant Surgeon of the Fourth Infantry Regiment. He served in the New Hampshire House of Representatives from 1826 to 1827, and was Canterbury Justice of the Peace from 1826 until his death. Harper served in the New Hampshire Senate from 1829 to 1831. He was President of the Senate and became Governor ex officio upon the resignation of Matthew Harvey, serving from February to June 1831. In 1830 Harper was elected to the U.S. House of Representatives as a Jacksonian and served two terms, 1831 to 1835. He then returned to his Canterbury medical practice, and also became involved in banking, serving as President of Mechanics' Bank of Concord from 1847 to 1856.

David E Harriman
Birth:
November 11, 1788
Plaistow, New Hampshire
Death:
Dec. 1, 1844
Hillsborough County, New Hampshire
Burial:
Hadley Cemetery
Weare
Hillsborough County,
New Hampshire

He was converted in 18 and seven and baptize by Rev. Timothy Morse in May. He soon began to teach and to preach. Then in 1808 he taught at Bangor, Maine and saw a good revival. Early in 1809 he returned to his hometown and married. He then moved to Candia where he was ordained on November 30, 1817.

John Sherman Harrington
Birth:
Dec. 17, 1846
Woodstock
Ontario, Canada
Death:
Dec. 30, 1911
Burial:
Pine Grove Cemetery
Farmington
Strafford County,
New Hampshire

He received an academic education, was converted at the age of 12, licensed March 5, 1870, and ordained by Rev's J. Ingram and George Donmocker on May 12, 1872. He graduated from Hillsdale Theological Seminary in 1880, and in July, 1881 took charge of a mission in Elmira, New York. Besides this church he pastored churches in New Hampshire, Michigan and had revivals in all of his pastorates. He was the father of Virgil Dewitt Harrington who ran the Oceanwave Hotel in Rye, NH.

Rev Josiah B Higgins, Sr
Birth:
Jan. 19, 1830
Livermore
Androscoggin County
Maine
Death:
May 16, 1878
Canterbury
Merrimack County
New Hampshire
Burial:
Canterbury Village Cemetery
Canterbury
Merrimack County
New Hampshire

Josiah B. Higgins, Chaplain for 12th Reg. NH Inf., received an invalid pension in December 1866, and his wife, Elizabeth M. Higgins received a widows pension, July 20, 1885. His service was from 1862-1865.

He was married May 1, 1852 to Eliza M. Cobb, and had two children, Josiah B., and Phebe E., who died young. His wife survived him a few years, dying in 1893, and leaving only one survivor of the family, John B., Jr. He had one brother, Franklin M., in the Army, who served in Co. "B" 5th NH Vol, and was mortally wounded at Fredericksburg, VA.

The following sketch was penned by Chaplain Higgins's son: Chaplain Higgins was converted in 1850 and baptized the following year in Biddeford, ME, by Rev. J.L. Sinclair. He became deeply interested in Christianity and the Sabbath school work at Bartlett. He was ordained in Feb. 1865, at Alton, by a special council called for that purpose, and was soon appointed Chaplain of the 12th Regiment in place of the lamented Ambrose. After the war he preached at Barnestead and Wolfeborough and moved to Canterbury in 1867 and became the minister of the Free Baptist Church there for three years. The rest of his ministerial labors were at Canturbury Centery and preaching to the scattered brethren at Northfield at the same time. He spent most of his later life with feeble and destitute churches, getting nor asking but a small salary and of time without any at all.

As a man he was cool and deliberate, persistent in what he thought was right and sueful, industrious and purdent in all his efforts and habits. He maintained himself and family chiefly by manual labor. He was a kind husband, indulgent father and was patriotic and highly esteemed by his fellow citizens. As a Christian he was sincere and devout. He cherished personal piety and practiced personal effort in his Christian work. His emotional manifestations were of a subdued, tearful character rather than noisy and ephemeral. As a minister he excelled at finding fields of destitution and want, where he bestowed the best efforts of his life. He was a reliable minister; his preaching was expository, though, spiritual and was not in vain.

Rev John Hill
Birth:
1790
Strafford
Strafford County
New Hampshire
Death:
Feb. 20, 1037
Burial:
Meredith Village Cemetery
Meredith
Belknap County
New Hampshire
Plot: Section 2, Range 9
Lot 4

Free Will Baptist Minister of Meredith. Married a Polly Watson born in Northwood, NH and mother of Elizabeth.
Ordained in 1822 to gospel ministry in the Free Baptist, and

resided in Meredith. A faithful minister, being true to the benevolent enterprises of the day. He was seen to fall, and before medical attendance could arrive, he had died.

Samuel Hill
Birth:
1784
Death:
Dec. 27, 1852
Loudon, New Hampshire
Burial:
Hill Cemetery
Loudon
Merrimack County,
New Hampshire

He was converted at the age of 18 and baptized at Canterbury, July 12, 1803 by Rev. Winthrop Young and remained a worthy member of the church there for 50 years. He was chosen a deacon in 1819 but was an ordained to the Free Will Baptist ministry in 1821 by the New

Durham Quarterly Meeting. He held offices of trust in his town; was a member of the legislature during Jackson's administration. Many were baptized by him. He died respected and honored.

Rev True Worthy Hill

Birth:
Nov. 8, 1825
Loudon
Merrimack County
New Hampshire
Death:
May 10, 1864
Ossipee
Carroll County
New Hampshire
Burial:
Canterbury Village Cemetery
Canterbury
Merrimack County
New Hampshire

His father moved to Canterbury when he was four years old. He remembered the helpful prayers of his pious mother. At the age of sixteen he was converted, and September 7, was baptized by Rev. M. COLE. After ten years of wavering he began to preach in July, 1852, having received a license from the Canterbury church with which he was connected. During the fall he labored with Rev. Uriah Chase in Buxton, ME.

January 1, 1853, he married Miss E. A. Mason of Canterbury. He moved with his wife to North Parsonfield in March, to study, meanwhile supplying the Brownfield church, at first fortnightly. The church revived, requested the Quarterly Meeting to ordain and settle him, which was done Feb. 22, 1854. During three years fifty-seven were added to the church. In April, 1857, he began the pastorate with the First Ossipee and Wakefield church which terminated with his death. Eighty were added to the church. He was a good mechanic and faithful preacher.

He was instantly killed in a saw-mill and was buried in Canterbury.

Marilla *Turner* Marks Hills

Birth:
Mar. 20, 1807
Vermont
Death:
Nov. 28, 1901
Dover,
Strafford County,
New Hampshire
Burial:
Pine Hill Cemetery, Dover,
Strafford County,
New Hampshire

She married Rev. David Marks, 20 Sep 1829, a Free Will Bapt. minister. They were involved in evangelizing, book publishing, and many works of the church.

died Sept. 11, 1859. Marilla then married Mr. Hills, who preceded her in death. She continued to live in Dover to the age of 93, a respected Free Will Baptist church woman.

She was elected treasurer of the Woman's Mission Society in 1848, and after the office of the treasurer was dissolved she became the corresponding secretary and remained such till the society dissolved. She edited and had published a Memoirs of David Marks, in 1846, taken from his diary and journals. She and her husband adopted and raised a niece, Julia Marks. Rev. David Marks died at age 44 in Oberlin, Ohio, where he is buried in Westwood Cemetery, Oberlin. Marilla and her husband were both active in the abolition causes at the Oberlin College. Marilla then married another esteemed FWB minister, Rev. Elias Hutchins, 26 Dec. 1846, a widower, in New Hampshire, where he pastored the Washington Street church in Dover. This union was not to endure for long as Rev. Hutchins' health failed in a few years and he

Abiel W. Hobbs
Birth:
1824
Death:
Feb, 6,1899
Burial:
Lakeview Cemetery
Freedom
Carroll County
New Hampshire

His ministry was in Maine.

Hiram Holmes
Birth:
October 3, 1806
Rochester, New Hampshire
Death:
May 1, 1863
Merrimack County, New Hampshire
Burial:
Presbury Cemetery
Bradford
Merrimack County,
New Hampshire

John C. Holmes
Birth:
Oct. 1, 1804
Death:
Sep. 13, 1866
Burial:
Old North Cemetery
West Nottingham
Rockingham County
New Hampshire

He consecrated himself to the Savior on November 8, 1827 and the next August was baptized at Crown Point by Rev. Enoch Place. Thereafter, he began to have meetings and appointments and on January, 1830 the New Durham Quarterly Meeting licensed him. He was ordained in Strafford, February 8, 1831 with Rev. B. S. Manson preaching the sermon. October 19, 1837 he married Miss Susanna Brown of Weare and in 1838 settled in Raymond. In 1839 he went to Bradford. During the next 20 years he made tours among the destitute churches of the Weare Quarterly Meeting. He was a member of the sixth, seventh, and eighth sessions of the General Conference.

He was ordained in Maine, Dec. 24, 1840 where he spent the majority of his ministry before moving to Barrington in 1853 near where he died. Spouse: Hannah F. Felker Holmes (____ - 1867).

Rev Leland Huntley
Birth:
Dec. 3, 1790
Marlow
Cheshire County
New Hampshire
Death:
Jun. 16, 1861
Campton
Grafton County
New Hampshire
Burial:
Blair Cemetery
Campton
Grafton County
New Hampshire

He was ordained in 1820, and ministered in Vermont and NH. Son of Isaiah & Elizabeth (Church) Huntley
Married 1st, Sarah Thomas in Brattleboro, Vermont on December 12, 1813
Married 2nd, Nancy F. Plummer on July 29, 1849

Henry B Huntoon
Birth:
Oct. 9, 1840
Salisbury
Merrimack County, New Hampshire
Death:
Jun. 18, 1909
Bristol
Grafton County, New Hampshire
Burial:
Lakeview Cemetery
Hampstead
Rockingham County, New Hampshire

He studied in the common schools and was converted in 1854. Licensed in 1883 and ordained in 1886 by the Wolfborough Quarterly Meeting. Besides his pastorates in that area he also served as a justice of the peace. Information from NH Vital Records at State Archives, Concord.

Rev Charles E. Hurd
Birth:
May 1, 1838
Death:
Jan. 27, 1911
Burial:
Pine Grove Cemetery
Gilmanton Ironworks
Belknap County, New Hampshire

His ministry was in Vermont. Enlisted in the US Army, Company D 4th NH Volunteers on 09/13/1861. Discharged 8/23/1865 Vermont and New Hampsire. Spouse: Anna A. Drake Hurd (1843 - 1908), Children:

Eugene Carlton Hurd (1866 - 1868), Charles Austin Hurd (1871 - 1909).

Father, into thy hands I commend my spirit."

Luke 23:46

Elias Hutchins
Birth:
Jun. 5, 1801
New Portland,
Somerset County, Maine
Death:
Sep. 11, 1859
Dover,
Strafford County, New Hampshire
Burial:
Pine Hill Cemetery, Dover,
Strafford County, New Hampshire
Plot: Sect. 4, Lot 91

He was baptized by his uncle, Rev. Samuel Hutchins, in 1818, and joined the church. He felt called to preach and on 8 Jan 1823, he was licensed at the age of eighteen. He purchased a horse and saddle and entered upon an itinerant ministry for two years in the Farmington and Edgecomb districts.

He was ordained a minister at Wilton Feb. 1, 1824.

He set out as an evangelist in Ohio and Indiana for two years, principally in Marion, Clark, and Warren Counties, Ohio, and in Dearborn and Switzerland Counties, Indiana. The winter of 1829 he spent among Free Will Baptists in North Carolina, where many slaves flocked to hear him preach.

He returned to New England in 1831 in New Hampshire and Maine. In Oct. 1833, he became pastor in N. Providence, Rhode Island, until 1838, when he went to Lowell, Mass.

He entered a pastorate of five years at New Market, N. H. He was elected Corresponding Sec'y of Foreign Mission Society, an office he held until his death.

In May 1845, he accepted a call to Washington St. church in Dover,

New Hampshire, and for a time was editor of the "Myrtle" and the "Gospel Rill" books used in Sunday School for children.

Dec. 26, 1846, he married Mrs. Marilla Marks, the widow of Rev. David Marks. He was 58 years at the time of his death. He died as he lived, a sweet, loving example of Christian trust. The heathen and the slave found a firm friend in him. He represented Ohio in the Second Gen. Conference, and was a member of the committee on an itinerant ministry. He served the General Conference in 1835, and 1850, on the committee on correspondence.

In 1842 he was president of the Home Mission Society, and in 1848-52 of the Education Society; in 1840-41 of the Sunday-School Union. He was a trustee 11 years, and corporator twenty-four years for the Printing Establishment.

He was converted to the age of 21; began to preach in 1846; and was ordained in 1854. He pastored a number of churches in the area where he was converted and ordained. He labored as an itinerant preacher and had revivals in his work. He was clerk of the Wentworth quarterly Meeting for a number of years.

Lorenzo Dow Jeffers

Birth:
Mar., 1821
East Haverhill
Grafton County
New Hampshire
Death:
Sep. 6, 1893
Grafton County
New Hampshire
Burial:
Number 6 Cemetery
East Haverhill
Grafton County
New Hampshire

Reuben Varney Jenness

Birth:
May 5, 1836
Strafford County, New Hampshire
Death:
Jun. 25, 1861
Dover
Strafford County,
New Hampshire
Burial:
Pine Hill Cemetery
Dover
Strafford County,
New Hampshire

Rev. Reuben V. Jenness, was the son of Nathaniel (1796-1882) and Lydia (Varney) JENNESS.He was converted at age fifteen, and baptized by his teacher, Rev. O.B. Cheney, joining the church in West Lebanon. He afterwards transferred his membership to Washington St. church, Dover, where his parents resided, and remained a devoted member for ten years. Feeling called to preach, he prepared for college principally at South Berwick, Maine, under the tuition of Dr. Grey. He entered Darmouth a year in advance, and graduated with high honors in 1859.He was married to Miss Emily C. Smith, of E. Randolph, VT, July 29, 1862, and was ordained Sept. 10, 1862, as pastor of the Pine Street Church in Manchester, not long before his failing health caused him "to go home to die." (i.e. Dover).He was a member of the FWB Foreign Mission Board, and especially excelled as a writer. He and had a bright future ahead of him, when he died at age 27 years.

Abner Jones

Birth:
Apr. 28, 1772
Worcester County,
Massachusetts
Death:
May 29, 1841
Burial:
Winter Street Burial Ground
Exeter,Rockingham County,
New Hampshire

He was a medical doctor, minister, and early church reformer. He was married 1804 to Damaris Prior, b. 6 Dec 1768 in Canaan, Conn., dau. of Clothier and Anna (Bramble) Prior.

We all have the same body, the same human flesh, and therefore we will all die.

Francis Kenerson

Birth:
Dec. 25, 1828
Albany, New Hampshire
Death:
Jan. 13, 1858
New Hampshire
Burial:
Chickville CemeteryCenter
Ossipee
Carroll County,
New Hampshire

He was 14 months old when his father died. At the age of nine, his mother moved with him to Great Falls. At 13 he returned to near the place of his birth to live with Joseph Bennett of Tamworth. At this time under, Rev. James Emery, experienced religion at age 14. Three years later he went to Hingham, Massachusetts to learn the trade of Carpenter. In the summer of 1851 he preached in Tamworth and vicinity till early in 1852 when he accepted a call to the Second Eaton church. Later he pastored a number of churches in the area. However, in November, 1857, his health failed and he preached his last sermon on November 29, at Tamworth in the very church where he preached his first sermon. Add age 29 years and 19 days.

Spencer Kenison
Birth:
1806
Death:
Mar. 10, 1884
Bartlett
Carroll County,
New Hampshire
Burial:
Garland Ridge Cemetery
Bartlett
Carroll County,
New Hampshire

Rev. Spencer Kenison, died in Bartlett, his native town, at age 75 years. He early married Miss Judith Hazelton, daughter of Rev. Samuel Hazelton, of Jackson, afterwards of Bethel, ME. He cleared a farm and made himself a comfortable home. At the age of twenty-seven, he was baptized by Elder John Pinkham, and with his wife united with the church in Bartlett. From this time he was the leader of the church, and for many years successfully ministered to them as a licensed preacher. A lady visitor having offered $200 toward the erection of a meeting house, he and his neighbors took their oxen, and went to the woods, cut the timber, and soon had a neat chapel built.In 1864 he was ordained, and continued the acceptable pastor of the church fourteen years. The last six years he was unable to work. He suffered severely before death came to his relief.

"I see Heaven open and Jesus on the right hand of God

We Are Made For A New Life And A New Body And A New Existence With The Lord.

Thomas Keniston
Birth:
Dec. 9, 1819
Woodbury, Burma
Death:
Dec. 25, 1901
New Hampton
Belknap County,
New Hampshire
Burial:
New Hampton Village
Cemetery
New Hampton
Belknap County,
New Hampshire

He studied one year at New Hampton and was converted in his 21st year. He was licensed in February, 1842 and ordained the next year by the Lisbon Quarterly Meeting at Bethlehem. He labored for a number of years in Maine and New Hampshire where he baptized more than 1400 people.

Rev Clarion Hazen Kimball
Birth:
Oct. 11, 1844
Hopkinton
Merrimack County
New Hampshire
Death:
Nov. 8, 1901
New York
New York County
New York
Burial:
Contoocook Village Cemetery
Contoocook
Merrimack County
New Hampshire

Civil War: Company E, 1st U.S. Sharps Shooters (Berdan's) & Company G, 18th New Hampshire Infantry

Clarion Hazen Kimball was the son of Hazen Kimball and Mary Ann Baker. He was a 17-year-old resident of Hopkinton, New Hampshire, when he enlisted as a private August 27, 1862, and was mustered into Company E, 1st U.S. Sharps Shooters. He was wounded in action at Locust Grove, Virginia, November 27, 1863. Private Kimball was promoted to corporal March 1, 1864. Corporal Kimball was mustered out October 16, 1864, to accept a commission as a 1st Lieutenant and was commissioned into Company G, 18th New Hampshire Infantry February 13, 1865. He was promoted to Captain and mustered out the same day, July 29, 1865. After the war he married Lucy A. Challen at Sangamon, Illinois, October 9, 1866, and became a minister. He lived for a time in Holyoke, Massachusetts. Clarion filed for a Civil War veteran's pension in Ohio February 19, 1892, and received application No. 1,092,811 and certificate No. 984,486. He later moved to New York City, where he died and Lucy filed for a widow's pension December 2, 1901.

He attended Bates College in 1867 and Morgan Park,(Ill) Theological Seminary, class of 1869. Licensed in 1867 Weare, NH and ordained in 1872 in Evansville, Wisconsin. He left the Free Baptist and became a Baptist.

Samuel Knowles
Birth:
1777
New Hampshire, USA
Death:
Nov. 15, 1850
Ossipee, Carroll County
New Hampshire
Burial:
Fall Cemetery
Ossipee
Carroll County,
New Hampshire

About 1830 he joined the Free Baptists and was ordained to their ministry. In 1832 he became a pastor at Sandwich, New

Hampshire. After a year and a half he moved to Eaton. In 1843 he went to Ossipee and continued to preach until a few months before his death of palsy.

He, That Has Learned To Pray, As He Ought, Possesses The *Secret* Of A Holy Life.

Elder Abner Leonard
Birth:
Nov. 4, 1777
Death:
Oct. 7, 1831
Hinsdale
Cheshire County
New Hampshire
Burial:
Oak Lawn Cemetery
Cheshire County
New Hampshire

A ministry connected to Dover NH Quarterly meeting, for about 10 years before his death.

Lincoln Lewis
Birth:
1799
Waterville, Maine
Death:
Apr. 21, 1858
Upper Gilmanton,
New Hampshire
Burial:
Sleeper Burial Ground
Gilmanton Ironworks
Belknap County,
New Hampshire

Rev. Lincoln Lewis was born to Thomas and Sarah (unk) LEWIS. He was ordained to the gospel ministry by the Free Will Baptist in 1822. He was married to Ruth P. (unknown m/n). He in 1824, was directed by the Lord in a vision to take a tour westward. He then passed through Parsonfield and was advised to go to Vermont, where Rev. Jonathan Woodman was laboring in great revival. On his way, through Franconia Notch, he says: "I turned aside into Ellsworth to spend a night with Elder Blake." He was overcome by a burden for that place, but the church there was divided, a separate meeting had been established, so he passed over the mountains. At Lisbon "I was kept awake most of the night by what seemed to me a voice saying, 'Ellsworth!--Ellsworth!' He returned the next day and discovered the church had met and prayed and were not surprised by his return. He then remained in the town a month; the church became united and enlarged; sinners were converted, and the same season a meeting-house was erected.

The Montville Quarterly Meeting sent Bro. Lewis with Rev. J. Farwell, in June, 1825, through the Exeter Q.M., and into "the Piscataquis country," to visit the feeble churches and explore the northern region between the Kennebec and Penobscot rivers. The report was favorable and led soon to the incoming of other ministers and the strengthening of the churches. The ministry of Rev. Lewis was confined to Maine and New Hampshire.

In April 1858, he was moving his residence at Upper Gilmanton, NH. He went for a second load of goods and was taken ill. Recovering somewhat, he completed the removal, but sank into a serious illness that night and expired in the morning in his 60th year.

Nathan Chase Lothrop
Birth:
Jun. 19, 1839
Norton
Bristol County, Massachusetts

Death:
Feb. 15, 1920
Bristol
Grafton County, New Hampshire
Burial:
Homeland Cemetery
Bristol
Grafton County,
New Hampshire
Plot: Sec. 20E Lot 7, Grave 7

Son of Solomon Lothrop and Fanny Chase. He was converted at the age of 17, after baptizing united with the church at Colton. He graduated from New Hampton institution in 1861 and from the theological school in 1864. He was ordained in the South Berwick, Maine, where pastored 18 months. Most of his pastorate was in the confines of the state of Maine. He married on November 16, 1865 to Sarah J Lovejoy of Laconia, New Hampshire.

Francis H Lyford
Birth:
September 19, 1820
Pittsfield, New Hampshire
Death:
1891
Burial:
Union Cemetery
Laconia
Belknap County,
New Hampshire
Plot: Section 392-E Grave 6

He was converted at the age of eight and studied at Pittsfield Academy, Clinton Grove Seminary, and the Friends Institution at Weare, New Hampshire. In 1859 he was licensed and in 1860 was ordained by the Strafford Quarterly Meeting, Vermont. His pastorates were in East Randolph and Thetford, Vermont; West Lebanon, Maine, Hampton, Laconia, and Meredith Ctr., New Hampshire; Haverhill, Massachusetts; Littleton, New Hampshire, to name a few. He was the author of the history of his hometown. In 1845 he married Miss Eunice Pickering and 1852 Miss Catherine S. Cox.

Josiah Magoon
Birth:
Jun. 25, 1758
East Kingston
Rockingham County,
New Hampshire
Death:
Feb. 5, 1841
New Hampton
Belknap County,
New Hampshire
Burial:
Magoon Cemetery
New Hampton
Belknap County,
New Hampshire
Plot: 4

He served his country faithfully in its struggle for independence and was present at Newcastle, Winter Hill and Ticonderoga. He accepted the Lord Jesus in the spring of 1780 and was baptized, joining a Baptist church. After he resided at New Hampton, in 1800, a remarkable revival was conducted by Rev. Winthrop Young. He was ordained in 1804 and remained faithful for nearly 40 years. Under the lead of brother Magoon, the church had almost yearly additions. For 10 years from 1833, 120 united with the church by baptism. He made occasional visits to Maine and Vermont, but most of his preaching was done in and around New Hampshire. He died at the age of 82

Note: Some information from the Inventory of New Hampton's Rural Burial Grounds, provided by the Town Clerk

Rev Benjamin Small Manson
Birth:
Mar. 5, 1802
Limington
York County
Maine
Death:
Dec. 7, 1879
Raymond
Rockingham County
New Hampshire
Burial:
New Market
Newmarket
Rockingham County
New Hampshire

Rev. Benjamin Small Manson was the son of John and Sarah (Small) MANSON.

He married Elizabeth Burnham, and after her demise, at age 66y he m. Elizabeth Hoyt, dau. of Alexander McClure.

Rev. Manson was a successful minister. He attended school at Effington. In 1825, after he had been preaching, he was ordained in at the Session of Parsonsfield Quarterly Meeting held at Hiram in August 1825.

He and his friend and former classmate, Rev. John Stevens, made a tour into Canada, a the request of Rev. John Buzzell. Money raised was seven dollars. They had a difficult time at first as the people thought they were 'frauds.' Finally, they recognized they were not like the other itinerant preachers they had encountered, and treated them kindly. They organized the McClure Church in Farnham, and stayed until winter, but he was in need of clothing for which he had no means of getting, he returned to Maine, with ten coppers in his pocket.

Rev. Jabez Fletcher, a successful minister in Maine was one of his converts.

He preached in Conway, NH, and engaged in teaching also.

John McClary
Birth:
1784
Epsom,
Merrimack County,
New Hampshire
Death:
Dec. 22, 1821
Epsom,
Merrimack County,
New Hampshire
Burial:
McClary Cemetery,
Epsom,
Merrimack County,
New Hampshire

He was killed almost instantly by the fall of a piece of timber from the frame of a shed under which he was standing. From his earliest youth he possessed a remarkable degree the affection of his friends, and the confidence of his fellow citizens. He was repeatedly elected a Representative from his native town in the Legislature of this State, and two years he was chosen a Senator, by the fourth district.

James McCutcheon
Birth:
Unknown
Death:
Sep. 2, 1855
Burial:
Old North Pembroke Cemetery
North Pembroke
Merrimack County,
New Hampshire

He was ordained in 1828 and his labors were in New Hampshire.

Asa Merrill
Birth:
Mar. 10, 1783
Stratham, N.H.
Death:
Nov. 13, 1860
Burial:
Congregational Cemetery
Stratham
Rockingham County,
New Hampshire

His conversion occurred 9, 1800 at the age of seventeen the Congregationalists and feeling call to the ministry he began study the pastor of his church. Through differing from his church he was baptized uniting with the Christian church. After preaching much in the southern part of the town he was ordained there May 9 1827. Rev Mark Fernald of Kittery, Me. preaching the sermon. He served this church till 1834 when he and the church united with the Free Baptists. During the eight following years he enjoyed frequent revivals and a number were baptized. In 1842 the church lost its visibility and he joined the Raymond church and preached there for several years. He afterwards removed his standing to the New Market church. To his first wife were born twelve children. Sarah P. is the wife of Rev. O. R. Bacheler missionary to India, another daughter married Rev JT Eaton a Methodist minister,

a son Daniel P. Merrill graduated from Dartmouth College in 1836 and for many years taught in Mobile Ala, As a preacher Brother Merrill was practical spirltual and rich in experience. Four years before his death he was prostrated with paralysis.

Nathan Merrill
Birth:
Unknown
Death:
Aug. 28, 1836
Burial:
Highland Cemetery
Rumney
Grafton County,
New Hampshire

He was ordained in the church at Gray, Me. by Randall and Tingley Oct 2 1787.

Stinchfield says,' Merrill ran well for a while. He has been useful to the church by occupying his proper gift which was of exhortation.'

He was pastor of Gray and New Gloucester church. When Stinchfield attempted to preach in 1793 he found little to help him.

Merrill encouraged the church in military display declaring that they might innocently engage in parades, which annoyed his ministerial brethren. The matter was brought before the YM for four years where it occasioned serious discord. Alienation finally ensued and Nathan Merrill ceased to co-operate with the people of his early choice.

Inscription:
"A soldier of the revolution"

Atwood B Meservey
Birth:
Sep. 30, 1831
Appleton,
Knox County, Maine
Death:
Feb. 21, 1901
Belknap County,
New Hampshire
Burial:
New Hampton Village Cemetery,
New Hampton, Belknap County,
New Hampshire,
Plot: 307

Mr. Merservey chose medicine as his profession and attended lectures at Bowdoin College. He decided to become a clergyman and came to New Hampton in 1855 to prepare for college. He graduated from the literary department there in 1857 and past three years in the study of theology, also attending for six months the Andover Theological Seminary; plus, lectures on physical geography and geology at Brown University. In 1861 he was ordained pastor of the Freewill Baptist Church at Meredith Village. In 1867 he became principal of the Seminary at Northwood, returning to New Hampton after a year, to become principal of that town's Seminary.

The school honored him by establishing the "Meservey Medal" in his name, which is still awarded to a person for outstanding contribution to the academic and social life of the school. Mr. Meservey received the degree of A.M. from Brown University and a Ph.D. from Bates College. Republican in politics he represented New Hampton in the State Legislature in 1867.

Nathan H Milton
Birth:
1811
Death:
1839
Dover, New Hampshire
Burial:
Trickey
Brookfield
Carroll County, New Hampshire
He was ordained for five years prior to his death and was able to preach the gospel until failed in health took his life.

Elder David Moody
Birth:
Dec. 3, 1804
Death:
Apr. 7, 1892
Burial:
Sutton Mills Cemetery
Sutton
Merrimack County
New Hampshire

Labored in New Hampshire, Vermont and Canada. He was a delegate to the first General Conference in 1827 at Tunbridge, Vt. He attended nearly thereafter and for 50 times to the Yearly Meeting.

Rev John Morse
Birth
Jun. 21, 1794
Otisfield
Oxford County, Maine
Death:
May 20, 1887
Whitefield
Coos County, New Hampshire
Burial:
Riverton Cemetery
Jefferson
Coos County, New Hampshire

Served in War of 1812.
The first ordained minister in Randolph, NH was John Morse. On March 18, 1816, he moved from Otisfield, Me., to Randolph, NH. He labored here a great many years.

In 1887 he was the oldest man living that was here when the town was Durand (Randolph, NH). He lived at Jefferson Mills some years, where he died in 1887, over ninety years of age.

Mr. Morse held meetings in Randolph and adjoining towns. In 1824 a Free Baptist church was organized in East Jefferson, and practically placed in his care. It consisted of a dozen or more members, and was in active operation while Elder Morse lived in Randolph.

In those days the people were poor, and the work of the minister was a labor of love. Religious meetings were held in schoolhouses and private dwellings. Ministers received little pay in money for services. On one occasion Father Morse walked twenty miles to attend a funeral, and then walked home again. He received a "present" of a pair of "feetings." He would get up early Sunday morning, walk to East Jefferson, hold three meetings, and then in the evening walk back to Randolph so as to be ready for his work Monday morning.

For miles the road lay through the wild, unbroken forest. One bright moonlit night a wolf trotted out into the road before him and sat down. The old man said he "was a little startled at first, but he grasped his stick more firmly and walked on. The wolf eyed him a moment and then trotted off." The old elder said "The exercise was good for him," and, said the man of ninety years as he straightened up, "I am better for it now." In 1837 Elder Morse moved from Randolph, and probably there has been no regular minister settled there since.

-History of Coös County, New Hampshire by George Drew Merrill; Syracuse N.Y.: W.A. Fergusson & Co., 1888.

Timothy Morse
Birth:
1765
Newbury, Massachusetts
Death:
Oct. 30, 1832
Burial:
South Newbury Cemetery
South Newbury
Merrimack County,
New Hampshire

In 1815 he was chosen to represent his town, and for several years said in the state legislature, and preaching as occasions offered. At one time three other ministers of Free Will Baptists denomination had seats in the legislature and boarded at the same house. When the days the work was ended they held religious meetings and evenings to as many as would come. Later, he abandoned his legislative career and gave himself wholly to the work as an itinerant preacher. His first tour was to Windsor, Vermont, where he was blessed in the gathering of the church of 60 members in 1822. In October, he returned to Rhode Island and added 42 to the Pawtucket church. Remaining there with the Rehoboth Free Communion Baptist Church, which was organized in 1777, and through his influence he so the church added to the Rhode Island Quarterly Meeting in August, 1823. In the summer of 1824, he saw large numbers converted in Randolph, Vermont. In July, 1825 he had good additions to the church in Danville. He remained in the area of Lyndon, Sutton and then removed to Strafford, Vermont where he had more than 300 people converted. His itinerant preaching took him into many states and regions. In October, 1830, he was an active and influential member of the fourth General Conference which was held at Greenville, Rhode Island. He had also been a member of the first General Conference. There was power in his presence which nothing could resist. He felt the power of Christ, and during his ministry baptize over 500 people.

Inscription:
Elder Timothy Morse
died Oct 30, 1832, aged 67 years. The gospel was his joy and song, E'en to his last breath, The truth he had proclaimed so long, Was his support in death.

William Alson Nealy
Birth:
Nov. 3,
Bolton
Chittenden County, Vermont
Death:

Jan. 28, 1890
Bristol
Grafton County,
New Hampshire
Burial:
Homeland Cemetery
Bristol
Grafton County,
New Hampshire
Plot: Sec. 15W, Lot 10, Grave 7

Rev. Wm. A. Nealy, studied at Green Mountain Seminary, and ordained Dec. 22, 1872. Pastored in Vermont, NY, and R.I. In 1887, took pastorate of Bristol, NH. Son of John Nealy and Sarah Cooper. William was a pastor of the Free Baptist Church in Bristol, Grafton, New Hampshire 1888-1890.

Samuel S Nickerson
Birth:
Sep. 24, 1835
Albany, New York
Death:
Apr. 2, 1930
Burial:

Sunny Side Cemetery
Grafton County, New Hampshire
He graduated from New Hampton Literary Institution in 1859 and from the theological department in 1863. He was licensed to preach on May 26, 1863 and ordained in Providence, Rhode Island on October 13, 1864 under the direction of the executive board of home missions. He was for four years a missionary to the Freeman in North Carolina and Virginia, from October 1863 to October 1867. He arrived at Roanoke Island, South Carolina and later was the society's first missionary to bear the word of life to this suppressed race. He pastored a number of churches in Vermont and also later in New Hampshire.He served faithfully the Free Baptist denomination from 1873 to 1918.

Jacob W. Nichols

Birth:
Nov. 25, 1823
Death:
Nov. 16, 1863
Burial:
Davis Meeting House Cemetery
Carroll County,
New Hampshire

Ordained, Effingham, March 1858, and pastor, First Church there, 1858-60;there to other churches before going to Effingham, July1863 where dies.

John Norris

Birth:
June, 1804
Death:
Aug. 15, 1870
Burial:
Glenwood Cemetery
Littleton
Grafton County, New Hampshire

He was married in October 1825 to Polly Sleeper. He was converted in March, 1828 and baptized in May by the Rev. Nathaniel Bowles joining the church in his town. Began to preach in 1839 and was soon ordained. He served for many years in New Hampshire and Vermont. After the death of Polly he married Mrs Ruth Nurse in December, 1861. He was thrown from a wagon receiving fatal injuries from which he died.

Josiah Norris, Sr

Birth:
Jul., 1779
Orange County, Vermont
Death:
Jan. 12, 1862
New Hampshire
Burial:
Wentworth Village Cemetery
Wentworth
Grafton County, New Hampshire

The son of Samuel Norris 1734 to 1816 and Huldah Bartlett 1734 to 1780 grew up in Corinth Vermont and continued living there until after marriage. He married, Aug. 25, 1801, Polly Adams, who was born in Moultonboro', N. H., Jan. 5,

1787. A Baptist minister he began when young, he continued his ministry a Freewill Baptist thru Vermont and New Hampshire. Went to Hanover New Hampshire in 1812. Went from Dorchester to Wentworth New Hampshire. A man who truly loved the Lord Jesus Christ and strong Christian.

Micajah Otis
Birth:
May 21, 1747
Barrington, Strafford County,
New Hampshire
Death:
May 20, 1021
Barrington, Strafford County,
New Hampshire
Burial:
Center
Strafford Cemetery,
Strafford, Strafford County,
New Hampshire

Otis was very instrumental in the development of the early northeastern Free Will Baptist Church, along with Elders John Buzzell, and other church fathers. He was dedicated to his church and its doctrine of Free Grace, Free Will, and Free Salvation to all. He preached until he died at nearly 74 years of age. In 1776, Micajah signed the Pledge to Support the American Revolution at Barrington, N. H. He was ordained a Free Will Baptist clergyman, and was a very respected and effective minister.

Rev Cumins Paris
Birth:
Sep. 24, 1810
Turnbridge, Vermont
Death:
Jul. 4, 1898
Burial:
Pine Hill Cemetery
Wolfeboro
Carroll County
New Hampshire

His father went from home when he was two yrs old, and he lived in the family of Thomas Button till his 17th year, his mother meanwhile dying. He was converted at sixteen and baptized by Rev. Geo S. Hackett, uniting with the Turnbridge church. He was at that time unable to read. At the age of twenty-one he went with his brother to work in Lowell, MA.

Here kind friends aided him and he was soon teaching a class in Sunday-school. At the age of 27, under the encouragement of his pastor, Rev. Nathaniel Thurston, he entered Strafford Academy and studied five terms.

Returning to Lowell, he married Eliza Martin, and soon after moved to Parsonfield, Maine, and entered the first class formed in the denomination in theology.

After a year of study he accepted a call to Eaton, NH. In three years he setled at Alexandria for two years and Andover NH one year. He then moved to Wolfborough, where, at the ripe old age, he now resides. He has been an acceptable minister and a worthy example.

Rev. Arthue C. Peaslee, the son of Rev. Isaac and Hannah Peaslee, was born in Sutton, N.H. He was converted at the age of thirty-three, and soon after, he attended school at New Hampton, NH with the ministry in view. He was ordained at Newfield, ME, May 5, 1868, where there had been a revival under his labors. In the fall of 1874, he attended the Vermont Yearly Meeting at West Topsham. He with others, remained and held a series of meetings which resulted in his being chosen pastor. The work prospered under his labors. He held seven pastorates, in nearly all of which there was revival interest.

A. C. Peaslee
Birth:
May 29, 1832
Death:
Jul. 1, 1876
West Topsham
Orange County, Vermont
Burial:
Old South Sutton Cemetery
Sutton, Merrimack County,
New Hampshire

Isaac Peaslee
Birth:
Jun. 9, 1795
Death:
May 11, 1884
Sutton
Merrimack County,
New Hampshire

Burial:
Old South Sutton Cemetery
Sutton
Merrimack County,
New Hampshire

He was an active Christian for more than seventy years. He was deacon for several years in the Sutton Church, and on Feb. 15, 1832, he was ordained a Freewill Baptist minister and entered upon his ministerial labors, which were mostly in the Weare Quarterly Meeting (District). He baptized nearly one hundred in his own town.

Inscription:
Rev. ISAAC PEASLEE
DIED
May 11, 1884AE 89 yrs.

Elder Dudley Pettingill
Birth:
Mar. 21, 1786
Weare
Hillsborough County
New Hampshire
Death:
Apr. 29, 1850
Thornton
Grafton County
New Hampshire
Burial:
Wildcat Cemetery
Thornton
Grafton County, New Hampshire

Rev. Dudley Pettengill, of Thornton, N.H., died, aged 63

years. He spent much time as itinerant preacher in the Middle and Western States. His labors were blessed at Sandwich, Meredith, New Hampton, and Thornton, in his own state. He visited and preached to all the churches in the Lisbon and Sandwich Quarterly Meetings. Revivals attended his labors.

He twice represented Sandwich in the Legislature of the state.

Son of Dudley S. & Mary (Heath) Pettingill and the husband of Hannah Boynton.

Charles L. Pinkham
Birth:
Nov. 18, 1841
New Durham
Strafford County, New Hampshire
Death:
Dec. 22, 1903
Burial:
Riverside Cemetery
Alton
Belknap County, New Hampshire

He studied at New Hampton and at Bates Theological School. He was converted in 1854. Licensed in 1874, and was ordained a Freewill Baptist minister, Oct 17, 1879, by Rev's E. Tuttle, J.C. Osgood, E.W. Ricker, G.M. Park and C.A. Bickford. He preached at Greene, ME, while in school (Bates) and received into the church forty. He is settled at Northwood, NH, where he baptized ninety-five and received into the church 127. He married Mary M. Muray Dec. 7, 1885. He has been several years treasurer of the New Hampshire Home Missionary Society.

C.O. G. 7th REG. NH VOLS.

Daniel Pinkham
Birth:
Jan. 7, 1799
New Hampshire
Death:
Jun. 25, 1855
Lancaster
Coos County

New Hampshire
Burial:
Wilder Cemetery
Lancaster
Coos County, New Hampshire

His name is enrolled in list of Freewill Bapt. ministers, in NH, and it gives the dates as here posted. "He was born in Madbury, NH, and labored in the ministry in NH, where he died.

Rev George H Pinkham
Birth:
Aug. 21, 1821
Jackson
Carroll County, New Hampshire
Death:
May 6, 1886
Lewiston
Androscoggin County, Maine
Burial:
Pine Street Cemetery
Whitefield
Coos County, New Hampshire
Plot: Section J, Lot 74

Rev. George H. Pinkham, son of Deacon Rufus and Mary Pinkham, was born at Jackson, NH, Aug. 21, 1821, and died suddenly at Lewiston, ME, May 6, 1886.
He studied in neighboring academies and completed his preparatory studies at Lancaster. He became a teacher and ever after maintained a connection with school interests. In youth he sought Christ and united with the

church at Jackson. He studied in the Biblical School at Whitestown, N.Y., graduating in 1849, and returned to Jackson, immediately beginning to preach. He was ordained at Tamworth Iron Works, Oct. 20, 1850, and remained at Jackson till 1853.

On October 12, 1851, he married Miss Susan E. Meserve of Jackson. He was pastor at Laconia two years, at Shelburne three yrs, and from 1858 at Whitefield 18 yrs, where a church edifice was built and many were added to the church. After a few months at Andover, he preached at Franconia two yrs, and at Meredith Centre 3 yrs. While at these places he taught fifty terms of school.

He moved to Lewiston to educate his children [Bates] preaching in the vicinity. He was superintendent of public schools thirty yrs. Three times he was county commissioner of schools in Coos County. He did much for popular education.

Rev Stephen Jefferson Pitman
Birth:
May 10, 1807
Meredith
Belknap County
New Hampshire
Death:
Jul. 31, 1876
Concord
Merrimack County
New Hampshire
Burial:
Blossom Hill Cemetery
Concord
Merrimack County
New Hampshire
Plot: Section: No. Addition,
Lot 27, Grave 1

He became a Christian in April 18, 1824, when seventeen years of age, and was the first person baptized by Rev D.[avid] Moody. May 25, 1830, at the age of twenty-two, he was ordained, and at once made a tour to Ohio, where he preached one year with success.

He was married in november 1833, to Olive B. French, and with his wife, and in company with rev's Dudley Pettengill and Gordon F. Smith, made another tour to Ohio and Indiana. After two years' absence he returned to Meredith. He taught school several terms. He labored faithfully as long as health permitted and led hundreds to the Saviour. He was a good scholar, a sympathetic and winning preacher, and modest, upright and true.

He was town clerk nineteen years. The last ten years of his life he resided in Concord. The last five years he was a great sufferer from an injury which finally caused his death

Inscription:
Rev. Stephen J. Pitman
Died
July 31, 1876
Aged 68
Olive B. His Wife
Died
May 31, 1909
Aged 96

David Marks Place
Birth:
Feb. 4, 1831
Strafford County,
New Hampshire
Death:
May 13, 1900
Strafford County,
New Hampshire

Son of Rev. Enoch Hayes Place. Served in Co. C, 324 Reg. Mass. Volunteers (Civil War).

Enoch Hayes Place
Birth:
Jul. 13, 1786
New Hampshire
Death:
Mar. 23, 1865
Strafford, Strafford County,
New Hampshire
Burial:
Center Strafford Cemetery,
Strafford, Strafford County,
New Hampshire, Plot: 83

Elder Place was a very active and respected minister in the northeastern Free Will Baptist movement, and rode horseback, or in a carriage, to attend far away meetings, where he was in demand as a speaker. He kept detailed records in journals which were transcribed by William E. Wentworth, entitled "Journals of Enoch Hayes Place, 1810-1865." These volumes were published by New Hampshire Society of Genealogists in Concord, New Hampshire in 1998. Church records and books note that he always had sound words and wise counsel. His work as a pastor or preacher was of an inestimable value to his church.

Joshua Quimby
Birth:
Nov. 5, 1766
Rockingham County,
New Hampshire
Death:
Mar. 31, 1844
Grafton County,
New Hampshire
Burial:
Sunny Side Cemetery,
Grafton County,
New Hampshire

He began to preach in 1792. He was ordained at Lisbon in 1800. He was at first a Baptist, and in 1811 he became a Free Baptist and was for more than thirty years pastor of that church on Sugar Hill and his pure Christian character and exemplary life carried an influence that can hardly be estimated. During his long ministry he doubtless officiated at more funerals and united more people in marriage than any other clergyman in town or who ever lived in town." (History of Lisbon, ME., by Guy S. Rix.) Others helping in this church were Rev. Josiah Quimby, Moses Aldrich, Timothy Tyler and Jonathan Bowles. They erected the first church building in 1829 which served until 1884 when a new one was erected. Records state it would seat 300-400 and valued at $3,500. From this small beginning, the Lisbon Quarterly meeting has arisen, numbering now about 1200 members. Rev. Quimby was a man of good judgment, and a Christian of sincerity and honesty. He was one of the most faithful and capable men of his day in church labors and difficulties. He travelled to sit on committees and councils. Many old church records mention his ministerial labors, such as "Rev. Joshua Quimby here (Whitestown Free Will Baptist) in 1816-17, forming a Religious Society and several persons were baptized." (Rev. Benaiah Bean, an associate, was the first resident minister of Whitestown. He traveled all over the North Country, preaching his faith, and organizing churches.

Moses A. Quimby
Birth:
Oct. 5, 1821
Lyndon,
Caledonia County, Vermont
Death:
Dec. 7, 1895
Pittsfield,
Merrimack County,
New Hampshire
Burial:
Floral Park Cemetery,
Pittsfield,
Merrimack County,
New Hampshire

He was a grandson of the Rev. Daniel Quimby. He received his early education at the Lyndon Academy and at Geauga Seminary, Ohio and took the three years course for the ministry at Whitestown, New York.

In January, 1842 he received license to preach and on December 3, 1845 he was ordained by reference Daniel Quimby, Jonathan Woodman and others.

He had the care of 10 different churches and his pastorates have averaged nearly 4 years. He closed the fourth pastorate with the Epsom church where he had been pastor for 10 years.

He baptized 160 converts. He was a member of two General Conferences and several years on the Home Mission Board. He built the new FWB Meetinghouse in Epson, N. H., 1854, which in 2007, has been moved into town and is being preserved for historical purposes.

Rev Daniel I Quint
Birth:
1836
Death:
1898
Eaton Center,
New Hampshire
Burial:
Conway Village Cemetery
Conway
Carroll County,
New Hampshire
Plot: Section B Block 3

He graduated from New Hampton Institution in 1869. His ministry was in New Hampshire, Vermont, and Maine.

Goram Parsons Ramsey
Birth:
Jan. 16, 1813
New Hampton,
Belknap County, New Hampshire
Death:

Aug. 23, 1876
Dover, Strafford County,
New Hampshire
Burial:
Pine Hill Cemetery,
Dover,
Strafford County,
New Hampshire,
Plot: Sect 4, Lot 91

Recording Secretary from 1843-44. He died in New Berwick about a year and a half after his last pastorate. Rev. O.T. Moulton conducted his funeral service. Rev's Hosea Quinby, his teacher, and Silas Curtis, who married him, assisted.

Vienna G. *Morrell* Ramsey
Birth:
Jan. 8, 1817
North Berwick
York ,County, Maine
Death:
Jan. 16, 1905
Dover, Strafford County
New Hampshire
Burial:
Pine Hill Cemetery
Dover, Strafford County
New Hampshire,
Plot: Sect. 4, Lot 91

At age seventeen he was converted and baptized by Rev. E. Fisk. Soon after, he attended school at Parsonsfield Seminary, a foundation he built upon to the end of his active ministry. He was ordained at Falmouth, Maine in Nov. 1839, and in June, 1840, settled in Epsom, New Hampshire. He spent one year at Hillsdale, Michigan, in charge of the Boarding Hall, and Mrs. Ramsey was lady principal. His pastorates always were fruitful, and under his ministry, churches obtained solidity, spirituality and efficiency. He was active in his denomination's Anti-Slavery Committee, of which he served as

At fourteen she taught school, and then went to Parsonsfield Seminary. She also studied at New Market Academy and Philadelphia Collegiate Institute. She married Rev. Goram P. Ramsey, a Free Will Baptist minister, in Aug. 1840. She was converted at age nineteen and soon became a contributor to the "Morning Star" and the Boston "Saturday Evening Post," and took a prize from the latter Aug. 5, 1840. She was a faithful helper to him in his several pastorates. When he served Hillsdale College in Michigan., she became the first lady principal there. She was deeply interested in foreign missions, and was very active in promoting the interests of the FWB Woman's Missionary Society. In 1851, she was elected as its president, serving several years. Before this, she was its corresponding secretary for three years. The Society often called upon her to deliver public addresses. Though she sacrificed her literary aspirations to home and parish work, her pen was not idle.

In God Is My Salvation And My Glory: The Rock Of My Strength, And My Refuge Is In God. (Psalm 62:7)

James Rand
Birth:
Sep. 15, 1815
York County, Maine
Death:
Dec. 24, 1888
Dover
Strafford County, New Hampshire
Burial:
Pine Hill Cemetery
Dover
Strafford County, New Hampshire
Plot: Section S-6 Lot 137 Grave 1

His father was John H. Rand, who was for more than 50 years a deacon of John Buzzell's church. He was converted at age 14 and baptized on January 18, 1830 by Rev. Elias Libby. He attended Parsonfield Seminary so he could teach. He was licensed from the Parsonlield quarterly meeting on September 11, 1833 and on September 25, 1840 was ordained by Rev. John Buzzell, B. S. Manson and others. He married on December 26, 1839 Miss Dorothy Fernald and they had four children. He pastored many churches in Maine and then in New Hampshire. Because he received meager offerings for his preaching he had to teach school and to engage in farming along with his work as a minister. He was for several years Pres. of the Home Mission Society and at one time member of its executive board. He also was a member of the Foreign Mission Board and was for 12 years its president. There were more than 16 ministers of the Free Will denomination present at his funeral.

Benjamin Odger Randall

Birth:
Feb. 7, 1749
Newcastle,
Rockingham County,
New Hampshire
Death:
Oct. 22, 1808
Burial::
Randall Cemetery,
Strafford County,
New Hampshire

He was the son of a sea captain. From age nine he followed his father at sea until age 18, when he tired of it, and at his request, his father put him as an apprentice to learn the art of sail making, which he followed until age 21. He served in the Revolutionary War as assistant commissary officer in the New Hampshire militia. He re-enlisted Sept. 10, 1776, and became a Sgt. in the company of Capt. John Calf., Col. Pierce Long's Regiment, New Hampshire Militia. A fellow officer, Joshiah Magoon, said that "He was accustomed to visit the sick and administer to them the consolations of religion; indeed doing largely the duties of a chaplain.

Thus many a desponding heart was cheered and made strong by his efforts."Upon hearing the Rev. George Whitefield, one of England's great preachers who came to America to preach, following his religious convictions, broke with his traditional religion of predestination and in 1780, founded the First Free Will Baptist Church of New Durham, New Hampshire, from which spread that church's beginnings in the northeast United States. His preaching was effective and he went near and far to preach, establish churches, and propagate the gospel. It was largely because of the exposures of the severe northeastern winters that his health failed and after 30 years of selfless service, died from lung disease, age 59 years, 7 mos. 27 days. The churches in that area erected a monument and slabs over his grave. His will was made 4 June 1808; a codicil was added 1 Oct; the will is on record at the county office.(taken from the book, "The Life of Elder Benjamin Randall, pub. 1827, Limerick. MA. By Eld. John Buzzell, a comtempary, who read Randall's notes and also had personal knowledge.) He was a great man who stood by his convictions and 'the Book.' His work, like the proverbial grain of mustard seed, grew to spread in all directions. He is remembered in books written about him and in many other ways after all these years. The large monument was erected a few years after his death by a grateful church to this great leader. Inscription: West side of tall monument reads "Benjamin Randall died October 22, 1808, 59 years, 8 months and 15 days. Founder of the Free Will Baptists.

Benjamin Walton Randall
Birth:
May 4, 1776
New Durham
Strafford County, New Hampshire
Death:
Sep. 24, 1843
New Durham
Strafford County, New Hampshire
Burial:
Randall Cemetery
New Durham
Strafford County, New Hampshire
He followed his father on the homestead. Parents: Benjamin Odger Randall (1749 - 1808) Joanna Oram Randall (1748 - 1826) Spouse: Sarah Titcomb Parsons Randall (1774 - 1860) Children: Josiah Parsons Randall (1801 - 1808)* Sarah Sewell Randall (1803 - 1805)

Sarah Titcomb Parsons Randall
Birth:
1774
Maine
Death:
Nov. 8, 1860
New Durham
Strafford County, New Hampshire
Burial:

Randall Cemetery
New Durham
Strafford County, New Hampshire

For several years prior to her marriage Sarah, historically known as Sally Parson, traveled on horseback doing missionary work and was a early evangelist with Benjamin Randall. Sarah's father threw her out of the house for being a despised Baptist, but finally relented and invited her home just before her marriage to Benjamin W. Randall, the son of the founder of the Free Will Baptist of the north. Her spouse was Benjamin Walton Randall. and their children were Josiah Parsons Randall (1801-08) Sarah Sewell Randall (1803 - 1805).

Rev Thomas F. Reynolds
Birth:
Jan., 1813
Death:
Aug. 27, 1864
Burial:
Chester Village Cemetery
Chester
Rockingham County
New Hampshire

His name/DOB/DOD, appears in Free Bapt. conference minutes as a minister having died in 1864, Chester, NH.

Caleb H. Richardson
Birth:
February 17, 1787
Death:
Apr. 25, 1868
Canaan, New York
Burial:
Wells Cemetery, Canaan
Grafton County, New Hampshire
He preached 35 years in Wilmot, Danbury, Grafton and vicinity. He took The Morning Star for over 40 years.

George Washington Russell
Birth:
Jun. 11, 1802
Woodstock

Grafton County, New Hampshire
Death:
Aug. 10, 1886
North Woodstock
Grafton County, New Hampshire
Burial:
Parker Cemetery
Grafton County, New Hampshire

He became a Christian when about 18 years of age and soon began to preach. He was ordained at Thornton Gore. He helped to form the Woodstock church, of which he continued a member until his death. The church edifice was built by him and in 1851.He was the son of Joseph and Mary (Robbins) Russell. He married 1st, Margery W. Pinkham. She died and he married Sally Mills.

Alvan Sargent
Birth:
1814
Union, Maine
Death:
1890
Burial:
Church Place Cemetery
Wilmot
Merrimack County
New Hampshire

He read theology and homiletics in Lowell, Maine. In 1844 and in 1845 he received license to preach. He was ordained in 1847 by the Weare Quarterly Meeting, in New Hampshire. He mainly pastored churches in New Hampshire. He baptized 203 converts, married 287 couples and attended 414 funerals. He was a Quarterly Meeting Clerk, a member of the General Conference and of the Home Mission Board. He served one term in the legislature. He was married in 1836 to Nancy Hayward who died and in 1880, then he married Miss Sarah Greely.

Seth Sawyer
Birth:
1808
Alton, New Hampshire
Death:
1892
Burial:
Riverside Cemetery
Alton
Belknap County,
New Hampshire

He was converted in 1831 and ordained in 1857. His labors were mostly confined to supplying churches where they had no settled pastor. He labored at Guilford village, new Durham, Middletown, Wakefield, East Alton, and Alton. He baptized among his converts a granddaughter of Rev. Benjamin Randall.

John Langdon Sinclair
Birth:
Jul. 10, 1809
Meredith,
Belknap County,
New Hampshire
Death:
Aug. 16, 1888
Burial:
Blossom Hill Cemetery,
Concord,
Merrimack County,
New Hampshire

He studied in the common school and at New Hampton he listened to the preaching of many of the fathers and before his twenty first year he was baptized by Rev B.S. Manson. In 1832 he was licensed. In 1833 he supplied the church in Lowell, Mass. and in May 1834 probably went to Dover, New Hampshire. On June 30 1835 he was ordained by Fisk Dana Hill and Pinkham and settled at Lynn, Mass. For nearly thirty years he was a member of the board of corporators of the Printing Establishment retained there for his business ability. He was twice president of the Home Mission Society.

He was President, Recording Secretary and Corresponding Secretary of the Sunday School Union. He was President of the Anti-Slavery Society. He was a strong and bold advocate of the right by prudence and economy he gathered in order that he might bestow upon the benevolent work of the denomination. From the time says Dr Brackett more than forty years ago when he as a pastor was laboring to build a church in Manchester and living on a meager salary gave the first hundred dollars of savings to our struggling Biblical School on to the day of his death he was a regular and liberal giver to all our benevolent causes. Many a poor student at New Hampton or elsewhere has received a regular donation from term to term to enable him to go on with his studies. Among the larger gifts already executed are $10,000 to Storer College. $1,000 to the Sinclair Orphanage in India. $1,000 to Hillsdale College. $1,000 to the Concord church and $500 to the Lake Village parsonage. No man in our denomination minister or layman with so small an income has given so much money to benevolent work.

Rev Hiram S Sleeper

Birth:
Jan. 11, 1811
New Sharon
Franklin County
Maine
Death:
Aug. 11, 1867
Meredith Center
Belknap County
New Hampshire
Burial:
Highland Cemetery
Belmont
Belknap County
New Hampshire
Plot: 6

Rev. Hiram S. Sleeper's father frequently conducted the social meetings of the church, and at age twenty, Hiram was converted and baptized by Rev. Samuel Hawthorn, uniting with the Freewill Baptist church. For several years he was engaged in teaching. In 1835 he married Miss Cordelia French. After hesitation, he began preaching in his native place and received license from the Farmington Quarterly Meeting in 1839. His itinerant labors for the next three years were blessed. In October 1842, his wife died.

In December he was ordained by his Q.M. In May 1845, he married Miss M. A. Dyer, and entered on his first pastorate with the Georgetown church. After supplying the Augusta church for six months, in May 1847, he entered upon two yrars' pastorate at Gardiner. He was then called to Monhegan, an island destitute of religious privileges fifteen miles from the mainland. Here in less than a year one-fifth of the inhabitants were converted. In 1850 he began a four years' pastorate at Phippeburgh. After spending fifteen years in preaching he entered the Biblical School at New Hampton (NH) but he was called away, before the first year's study was completed by the church in Upper Gilmanton. Here he entered in Novemter 1855, upon a successful pastorate of five years. He spent two years at Bristol, four yrs at Loudon, and then began his last pastorate, at Meredith Centre where his health failed. After weary months of suffering he passed away, and was buried, according to arrangements made years before, by the request of his loving parish, at Upper Gilmanton. As a preacher he ws earnest and fearless. He was a friend and supporter of all the benevolent enterprises of his denomination, and took deep interest in his country's welfare. He was delegate to General Conference.

How precious is the dust of a believer!

Rev Alpheus D Smith
Birth:
Aug. 25, 1813
Lebanon
Grafton County
New Hampshire
Death:
Feb. 9, 1886
Canterbury
Merrimack County
New Hampshire
Burial:
Union Cemetery

Laconia
Belknap County
New Hampshire
Plot: Lot 169-1

His father, Dr. Alpheus Smith, was a surgeon's mate in the War of 1812, and died after a few month's service, November, 1813. His mother was Mehitable (Foster) Smith. Dr. Smith was born in R.I., educated at Providence and practiced medicine awhile in that state. At the time of his death the subject of this sketch was two months old. When three or four yrs old, his mother moved to Hartford, VT. At fourteen he was "bound out" until he became of age. He made the most of his winter school privileges.

He became a Christian when seventeen years of age, was baptized at Norwich, VT, May 12, 1830, by Rev. H.N. Plumb, and united with the church in Hartford. On Nov. 5, 1834, he preached his first sermon in the dwelling-house of Reuben Paine. He then spent several weeks with Rev. Nathaniel Bowles, traveling and preaching among the churches of the Vermont Yearly Meeting (Freewill Baptist). Here he formed a taste for itinerating, which continued during his life. At the advice of Mr. Bowles, he visited a neighborhood in W. Corinth, VT, where about 25 were converted. During the next few months he travelled in 13 towns in VT as far north at Lyndon. In May 1834, he was licensed at the Strafford Quarterly Meeting (QM). Rev. J. Woodman being chairman of the examining committee. In the spring of 1836, in company with Ezekiel True, he attended Parsonfield Seminary. These two students preached nearly every Sunday from six to ten miles away. After the summer school he went to the town of Stowe, in northern VT, accompanied by Brother True. A revival followed with forty or fifty conversions. He then went to Corinth, much exhausted and afflicted with a severe cold which resulted in typhoid fever.

He was ordained at a session of the Corinth Q.M. June 22, 1837, held at that church.

In July he became pastor of the Dover church, NH.

He was married to Miss Emily B. TRUE, sister of Rev. Ezekiel True. In the autumn while engaged in extra meetings at New Market, he was taken with severe bleeding of the lungs. In the spring he returned to Corinth, VT and the following winter built him a house and remained there several years. He soon recovered so as to preach regular.

His wife Emily, died Oct 18, 1872, and later he married the widow of Charles Clough, Mary E. (Osgood) Clough.

**Show thy vacant tomb, and let,
As of old, the angels sit,
Whispering, by its open door:
"Fear not! He hath gone before!"**

Rev. I. D. Stewart, D. D.

Rev Isaac Dalton Stewart
Birth:
Dec. 23, 1817
Warner
Merrimack County
New Hampshire
Death:
Jun. 7, 1887
Dover, Strafford County
New Hampshire
Burial:
Henniker Cemetery
Henniker, Merrimack County
New Hampshire

Isaac Dalton Stewart, D.D., was born the second child, to John and Hannah (Dalton) and the eldest son of their six children. His father's ancestry was Scotch, and several members of the family came to this country between 1725 -1760. His mother was a descendant of Philemon Dalton, who came from England in 1635 and settled in Mass. His home was on a farm of 200 acres among the hills of Warner, NH, and commanded a wide prospect extending into more than twenty towns.

Isaac D. attended the district school of 25 scholars before he was five years old.

In Sept. 1834, when nearly seventeen years, he fully decided to live "with reference to God's claims." His mother had been fatally injured by being thrown from a wagon, and her death, with attendant circumstances, her prayers and instructions vividly brought to mind by this event were powerful motives in his conversion. During the next eight yrs he mostly taught school or studied in preparation for his life work. He was in Hopkinton Academy, at time of his conversion, and after this in Ohio about two years from 1836, engaged in teaching. While there he chose the profession of law, then returned to NH pursued his studies in the academy at Henniker until the spring of 1840, when he turned his attention to the ministry. He was convinced of his call to the ministry and 1841, entered the Biblical School at Parsonfield, ME, under instruction of Rev. Moses M. Smart. He then attended New Hampton Theological School, and studied under the Baptists. In the spring of 1842, he was principal of Henniker Academy, having as pupils, Edna Dean Proctor, and James W. Patterson, afterward US Senator. In June he attended for first time a session of the NH Yearly Meeting and from that time for forty-five years till the session that began on the day of his death he was absent but twice.

He began to supply the church at Meredith Village church and became pastor, receiving $140 per annum salary. Her he baptized 25 after a revival.

He was ordained to the ministry in the Free Will Baptists, Feb. 2, 1843; Rev. E. Fisk preached the sermon, and Dr. Simeon Dana, and Rev's Thomas Perkins and Samuel Thompson assisted the services. Soon after, Feb. 8, 1843 he married Miss Elizabeth G. Rice of Henniker. April 1844, he began an eight-year pastorate at Laconia, NH where his only child, a daughter, Frances M. was born. He pastored many other places and into Ohio for his health, but returned, and became teacher of mathematics in New Hampton Institution.

In Nov. 1865, he accepted a call to Boston, and in April 1867, he became pastor of the noted Washington Street church in Dover, NH.

He made strenuous exertions on behalf of Storer College in VA due to a crisis that had arisen there. The Washington church sold their meeting house to the FWB Printing Establishment in Jan. 1868, he gave his time and strength to building a large brick church which they since occupied. Large spiritual prosperity attended his labors as pastor of this church. But in July 1873, he became agent of the Printing Establishment, having already been a member of its board of corporators fourteen years, and carefully managed the affairs of it. Rev. Stewart was clerk of the YM seven years, and several times its moderator. He was delegate to three or more General Conferences before 1868, after which he was standing clerk of the Gen. Conf. until his death. He was rec. Sec'y of the Home Mission Society 3 yrs and on its Exec. Committee for several years, and held similar positions in the Education Society, and was fourteen yrs secretary of the Anniversary Convention.

He filled extended terms as trustee of Bates College, Storer College, and Hillsdale College (MI). Assisted by Rev. Silas Curtis, he prepared for publication the first volume of the *"Minutes of the General Conference.*

He wrote valuable chapters for *the "Centennial Record."* The *"Ministers' Manual,"* pub. by the Printing Estab., is his work.

A most valuable contribution to his Free Will Baptist denomination was his *"History of the Free Will Baptists," Vol 1,* pub. 1862, at Dover, NH. Preface: "In 1853 the Printing Establishment appointed a committee to collect materials for a history, and after five years' effort, the collection, consisting of books, records, papers, and reports from ministers, churches, Quarterly and Yearly Meetings, was placed in the hands of Rev. I.D. Stewart, to prepare the work for publication."

In his bio, "Bro. Stewart was distinguished for strict integrity, self-sacrificing devotion, efficiency, promptness and thoroughness; but to those who knew him as pastor and associate these traits became doubly impressive and influential through his uniform gentleness and unaffected kindness of heart.

Elizabeth G. Rice Stewart
Birth:
Jun. 7, 1819
Henniker
Merrimack County
New Hampshire
Death:
Mar. 21, 1908
Massachusetts

Burial:
Henniker Cemetery
Henniker
Merrimack County
New Hampshire

Elizabeth G. Rice was mar. to Rev. Dr. I.D. Stewart, Feb. 8, 1843. She was mother of one child, Frances M., b. Laconia, NH. She no doubt led an interesting life married to her husband who moved many times during his teaching, preaching assignments.Spouse: Isaac Dalton Stewart (1817 - 1887)

Levi Streeter
Birth:
Apr. 10, 1806
Lisbon, New Hampshire
Death:
Jul. 22, 1886
North Lisbon, New Hampshire
Burial:
Glenwood Cemetery
Littleton
Gratton County, New Hampshire

He was a member of the Littleton church. He was born within the bounds of the Lisbon Quarterly Meeting.

He was licensed in 1826 and ordained 1881. His ministry was in New Hampshire.

He was a Christian over 40 years and 35 of those who use as an ordained minister.

Hiram Stevens
Birth:
December 12, 1806
New Chester, New Hampshire
Death:
Jun. 6, 1880
Meredith village,
New Hampshire
Burial:
Meredith Village Cemetery
Meredith
Belknap County, New Hampshire

He began to hold meetings when he was about 15 and soon went to New York and for most of the time until 1827 preached with success in the various adjoining towns in the area. In April, 1825 he was licensed by the Ballston Christian church. He returned to New Hampshire in 1827 and in the following spring began to preach in Lowell as a Free Baptists. In June he was received as a licensed preacher by the New Hampshire Yearly Meeting at Strafford and in August of the next year he joined the New Durham Quarterly Meeting. He was ordained at Canterbury on January 20, 1830. He gathered a church at Lowell. He preached as an evangelist in different towns with much success. At Meredith Village there were many added to the church. After this he was at Farmington and

Dover. He in 1852 he started the Belvedere mission in that part of the area called Centreville. He ultimately returned to Meredith Village where he spent his last years.

Edwin Byron Stiles
Birth:
January 16, 1860
Albany, Vermont
Death:
1917
New Hampshire
Burial:
Woodstock Cemetery
Woodstock
Grafton County, New Hampshire

He graduated from Bates College in 1885 and from Andover theological Seminary in 1888. He was licensed to preach in 1886 and ordained on February 15, 1888 by the Massachusetts Association. On June 25 he married miss Idaho in. Tucker a college classmate and after it became settled that the foreign mission field was to be his home. They sailed in November as missionaries to India.

Ada Henrietta Tucker Stiles
Birth:
1864
New Hampshire
Death:
1927
New Hampshire
Burial:
Woodstock Cemetery
Woodstock
Grafton County, New Hampshire

The wife of Rev. Edwin Byron Stiles. They married in Lowell, Massachusetts on June 25, 1888. She served as a missionary to India with her husband Edwin.

Rev William Swain
Birth:
May 13, 1788
Brentwood
Rockingham County
New Hampshire
Death:

Sep. 21, 1865
Burial:
Knowlton-Edgerly Cemetery
Chichester
Merrimack County
New Hampshire

William Swain, married Miss Sally Drake, Nov. 22, 1810, and in 1816 moved to Pittsfield, where he became connected with the Free Baptists. He was ordained June 7, 1827, and next year he moved to Chichester where he raised up a church of which he remained the beloved pastor nearly forty years till his death. It was said by one who knew him, "If the New Testament should be lost to the world, from the chambers of his own retentive memory he could have replaced it. He was strong in faith and an example to to his flock. Rev. E. Tuttle attended his funeral.

Rev Levi B. Tasker
Birth:
Mar. 21, 1814
Strafford County
New Hampshire

Death:
Aug. 29, 1875
New Hampshire
Burial:
Baptist Burial Ground
Center Sandwich
Carroll County
New Hampshire

Rev. Tasker entered Strafford Academy at the opening in 1834, and continued four years. He had saved $300 by working at the shoemakers' trade, which he now used for his education. In 1837 he was converted. The prayers in his behalf when he became a Christian included the petition that he might be called into the ministry. For seven years he fought his convictions, and the remembrance of these prayers made the conflict more distressing. Unable to study, he left school and returned to his trade. As a layman, he was very active in the church in Northwood, which he joined at his conversion. He served as clerk and superintendent of the Sunday school. While a student he sent out the first call for a county temperance society and was active in its organization. He was excluded from his church becaused he opposed its withdrawal from the Rockingham Quarterly Meeting (QM). in hostility to the strong anti-slavery stand which the QM had taken but he was afterward restored.

In 1845 he yielded to his convictions, was licensed and was soon after ordained. He itinerated for a few years, and then settled in

Sandwich in 1848. In that field he spent thirteen years out of the next twenty-six. Three times he went to other fields and as often returned. He once went to his native town and resuscitated the church at Bow Lake. Eight or nine years before his death he settled at Lyndon, VT and did valuable work there and in Wheelock Q.M.

The Lyndon Institution was greatly indebted to him at its establishment. He was clerk of the Sandwich Q.M. and of the New Hampshire Yearly Meeting (YM). many years. He was corporator of the Printing Establishment seven years and a member of its executive board, also of the executive boards of the Education and Home Mission Societies, of the latter about twenty years clerk. He was an excellent preacher, a good pastor, a wise counselor, and a worthy citizen. He had taken charge of the church in Sutton, VT, but after several months his failing health led him back to Sandwich, where he retained a pleasant home.

Rev Ezekiel True
Birth:
Jun. 5, 1811
Corinth Center
Orange County
Vermont
Death:
Feb. 18, 1883
Rochester
Strafford County
New Hampshire
Burial:
Rochester Cemetery
Rochester
Strafford County
New Hampshire

Rev. Ezekiel True was born Corinth, VT, June 5, 1814. He was fond of books in youth and became a Christian at fourteen, being baptized and received to church membership two years later. He began to preach at the age of twenty-one and was ordained at a session of the Corinth, VT Quarterly Meeting (QM) in 1837. In Jan. 1838, he began his first pastorate in Portsmouth, NH. which continued about 3 years and

100 were converted. He afterward held pastorates in Wells,ME; Ashland,NH; So Berwick,ME; Pittsfield,NH; Gilford,NH; Farmington, NH; Saco, ME; and Rochester,NH.

At the time of his death, which occurred suddenly, he was preaching at Walnut Grove, near Rochester. All his pastorates were marked by faithful service and gratifying results. He served as City Missionary during part of his stay in Portsmouth, and was a member of the school committee in most of the towns in which he lived.

He was the founder of the Rochester church, and the edifice erected soon after his death was named in honor of him, the "True Memorial Church."

His active intellect, fervor and power as a preacher, warmth of sympathy and congenial manners, made for him hosts of friends wherrever he lived.

Job C. Tyler
Birth:
unknown
Death:
Sep. 1, 1879
Canaan,
New Hampshire
Burial:
Wells Cemetery
Canaan
Grafton County,
New Hampshire

He was ordained in 1833 and preached constantly in the towns of Canaan, Orange, Grafton, and Hanover, until by old age. He was a main instrument of revivals in other places especially in East Andover and for years he preached in his own dwelling house. He died at 80yrs. 6mos.

Bartholomew Van Dame

Birth:
Jun. 21, 1807 Netherlands
Death:
Apr. 3, 1872
Nottingham,
Rockingham County,
New Hampshire
Burial:
Epping Central Cemetery,
Epping,, Rockingham County,
New Hampshire

He came over with Capt John C. Long of Portsmouth, New Hampshire in 1819 and came to Epping with Josiah Clark Feb 14, 1822 and served his time with Ensign John Dow from Feb 10, 1824 to June 21, 1828. He suffered many accidents, one that permanently maimed his right arm. In his sixteenth year with John Dow. He began to read, and thirsting for knowledge, he had in Epping acquired a good education. He studied under Dr. Timothy Hilliard, who deeply impressed him and with whom he went on lecture tours. After three terms with Dr. Hilliard he taught three months in Epping, having forty pupils. Again he entered the school of Dr. Hilliard, sometimes acting as his assistant while practicing the most rigid economy. In 1830, he entered New Hampton Institution. He studied mathematics of which he was fond. On Aug. 14, 1830, he was baptized in Epping by Rev. Israel Chesley of Durham. He prepared and published 500 copies of a small hymn-book, partly original. He studied Latin with, Dr. Hilliard, and

he taught for three years to gather funds and uniting meanwhile with the Greenfield FWB church under Pastor Rev. John Kimball, where his membership remained until his death. He studied Greek under John D. Philbrick, afterward superintendent of the Boston public schools, and read the classics. He entered Strafford Academy in 1835, having Prof. John Fullonton as his classmate in Latin and Greek. He entered the Congregational Theological Seminary at Gilmanton Center soon after his graduation at Strafford. After teaching in various places in Maine and New Hampshire in 1837, he came to Epsom, New Hampshire to supply the vacant pulpit in connection with his teaching, and having a revival he held seventy meetings. Here, April 10, 1838, he was ordained by Arthur Caverno, John Kimball, and Daniel P. Cilley. During forty years, he taught thirty years in all. He was ever a promoter of education. He came and went visiting Washington and the South, looking on statesmen, while thinking and studying about the magnitude of the offense of slavery under his own keen observation. He went to gatherings, sacred, secular, and patriotic, delivering speeches abounding with information, and rendered interesting and fascinating by the quaint individuality of the man.He could hold an audience's attention for hours.

He left a manuscript of 10,000 closely written pages composed since 1834, among them a hymn-book, dictionary, chemistry, arithmetic, geometry, grammar, and lectures on anti-slavery and temperance.

Having willed to several churches and to the benevolent enterprises of his denomination his personal effects, he wrote in his epitaph: "This world I leave without a debt behind,"

Rev William H. Waldron
Birth:
1817
Farmington
Strafford County, New Hampshire
Death
Jan. 6, 1894
Burial:
Waldron F01-5B1
Farmington, Strafford County, New Hampshire

Studied at Parsonfield Seminary in Maine and began to preach, 1842. Ordained Jan. 26, 1848. Pastored in Mass., Maine, Rhode Island, New York and New Hampshire.
Inscription:
Hus. of Mary S. Waldron
& Sarah Clough

Granville C Waterman
Birth:
May 4, 1835
Booth Bay, Maine
Death:
1927
Burial:
Union Cemetery
Laconia, Belknap County, New Hampshire
Plot: Section 87, Grave 6

He was a son of the Rev. Dexter Waterman. He was converted when 16 years of age and received his education at Litchfield Liberal Institute and Bowdoin College. He received license to preach in 1863 and was ordained on March 23, 1869 by Rev.'s D. Jackson, H. Perry, D. M. Stuart, George H. Ball and A. Aldrich. He held pastorates in New York. New Hampshire and baptized about 60 converts. For some years he was principal at Pike Seminary, New York. He held important positions on the denominational boards. From 1881 to 1888 he was editor of the Sunday school quarterly's and for years has been prominent in Sunday school work. On April 28, 1861 he was married to Miss Julia Mansfield and after her death on December 4, 1873 he married Marietta Stewart. He had several years as a successful professor in Whitestown Seminary and has been active in literary and missionary work.Note: Interred 25 Apr

Rev Elijah Watson
Birth:
Sep. 2, 1777
Nottingham
Rockingham County
New Hampshire
Death:
Nov. 2, 1837
Burial:
Old North Church Cemetery
East Andover
Merrimack County
New Hampshire

Son of Nathan Watson and Ruth Hinkson. m1 Miriam Sawyer on March 9, 1798, m2 Rhoda Felch on Sept 28, 1817, m3 Betsey Goss in 1854. Died aged 80 years 2 months Source:
- History of the Town of Andover, New Hampshire: Genealogies By John Robie Eastman (1910)

Rev Horace Webber
Birth:
Apr. 19, 1807
Lyman
Grafton County, New Hampshire
Death:
Feb. 21, 1872
Ossipee
Carroll County, New Hampshire
Burial:
The Stevens-Burleigh Site
Ossipee
Carroll County, New Hampshire

Horace Webber was a Freewill Baptist minister throughout the state of New Hampshire. He baptized more than 600.

Nathaniel Marshall Webster
Birth:
Unknown
Death:
1827
Burial:
Baptist Burial Ground
Center Sandwich
Carroll County, New Hampshire

Rev. Nathaniel Webster, of Tamworth, N.H., was ordained in 1801, a Freewill Baptist minister, and for many years did good work in his itinerant ministry in Maine and New Hampshire. In 1804, he visited Richmond, N. H., in company with Timothy Morse, and having baptized thirty or more converts, gathered and organized a church. In 1809, he organized a church at Wells, ME.

Rev Dearborn Wedgwood
Birth:
Sep. 29, 1810
Death:
Oct. 7, 1876
Farmington
Strafford County, New Hampshire
Burial:
Pine Grove Cemetery
Farmington
Strafford County, New Hampshire

Ordained in 1844. His wife and seven children survived him. She was bn 1814, and d. in 1887, age 73y,at Boston, MA, but have not located her grave. Parents were Samuel and Betsey Deland. If found, please link to her spouse.

Abel Wheeler
Birth:
Unknown
Death:
Mar. 13, 1870
Burial:
Center Haverhill Cemetery
North Haverhill, Grafton County,
New Hampshire

When about twenty-six years of age he became a Christian. About twelve years afterwards he moved to Haverhill and was one of the original members of the Freewill Baptist church there. He was licensed to preach by the church, and soon after was ordained at Lisbon Quarterly Meeting in 1832. He preached Christ faithfully in several towns until obligated by failing health to retire from the work. He was much respected for his honesty as a man and his consistency as a Christian.He was married to Lipah Wakefield, 23 Oct. 1814, at Newport, NH. In census there is child in 1850 NH census, Lonia M. Wheeler, b. abt 1836.

Frederick L Wiley
Birth:
March 16, 1836
Maryland, New York
Death:
1926
Burial.
Union Cemetery
Laconia
Belknap County, New Hampshire
Plot: Section 505, Grave 1

He received his preparatory education at Whitestown Seminary, New York and graduated from the theological school at New Hampton, New Hampshire in 1868. In 1865 he received license to preach and September 8, 1868 he was ordained by Rev's. J. Mariner, L. B. Tasker, and others. He was married in 1862 Miss Lena L. Smith who died in 1863. In 1868 he was again married to Miss Rebecca Weeks. He held pastorates at Sheffield and Sutton in Vermont; Bath, Maine; Concord, Whitefield and Gilford, New Hampshire. He received 250 people into churches, 127 by baptism. He was a member of the General Conference of 1877. He has for several years been editor of The Messenger. He also wrote *The Life and Influence of Benjamin Randall;* and *A History Of Free Will Baptists.*

Note: Interred 14 Apr 1926

Otis F. Willis
Birth:
1810
Hanover, New Hampshire
Death:
May 8, 1865
Franconia, New Hampshire
Burial:
Willow Cemetery
Franconia
Grafton County, New Hampshire

He was converted in March, 1830 and was baptized by Rev. David Cross. He began to hold meetings, traveling mostly in Vermont and New Hampshire and had several revivals. In 1832, he was licensed by the Strafford Vermont Quarterly Meeting. The same year he moved to Lyndon, Vermont to preach a part of the time at Daniel Quimby's church. In 1834, he was ordained at the request of the church in settled as pastor. In 1835 he entered on a six years pastorate with the church and Sugar Hill,

New Hampshire where revivals were enjoyed. In 1841, he moved to Potsdam, New York and in the company of Rev. M. Cole labored in an extensive revival where a church was organized at West Potsdam where he pastored for two years. In 1849, he returned to Sugar Hill. He began to practice medicine in 1838. The ministry was down neglected for this calling, for the rest of his life. He preached but occasionally and on funeral occasions. He was often heard to regret that he had not followed the work of the ministry.

Though policy teacheth us not to trust our enemies, yet piety teacheth us to love them.

Ephraim Winslow
Birth:
May 6, 1805
Nottingham
Rockingham County
New Hampshire
Death:
Jan. 28, 1872
Pittsfield
Merrimack County, New
Hampshire
Burial:
Quaker Cemetery
Pittsfield, Merrimack County
New Hampshire

He was ordained in Nottingham, 1846 and pastored it 1845-57. He went to South Candia, gathered a congregation and had a successful work. They went to Northwood, and later to Barnstead where he died.Marriages: Mary Tucker - 24 MAY 1824. Sally Greene - 18 MAR 1827 in Pittsfield, NH.

Christ Has Led the Way

Rev Thomas Wyatt
Birth:
Sep. 5, 1818
Campton
Grafton County, New Hampshire
Death:
Oct. 24, 1895
Bristol
Grafton County, New Hampshire
Burial:
Blair Cemetery
Campton
Grafton County, New Hampshire

Son of Thomas Wyatt and Martha P Wilson. Married twice: 1. 4 Mar 1836 to Sarah Ann (Clark) Sawyer. To thier union was born 6 children: George C Wyatt, Ellen A Wyatt, Nathaniel E Wyatt, Martha L Wyatt, Sarah Evangeline Wyatt, and Horace F Wyatt. 2. 14 Dec 1876 New Hampton, Belknap, New Hampshire to Mary Noyes (Hammond) Johnson. No children born of their union. Thomas was a farmer and Freewill Baptist Clergyman.

Thomas had resided in Campton, Grafton, New Hampshire; Thornton Gore, Grafton, New Hampshire; Rumney, Grafton, New Hampshire; Bridgewater, Grafton, New Hampshire; and from 1887 in Bristol, Grafton, New Hampshire.

Winthrop Young
Birth:
1753
Barrington, Strafford County,
New Hampshire
Death:
Jan. 6, 1832
Canterbury,
Merrimack County,
New Hampshire
Burial: Hackleboro, Canterbury,
Merrimack County,
New Hampshire

Rev. Young became a school teacher, and after having lived in other locations, moved to Canterbury. Here he was chosen captain of the militia, and his tall, fine figure and courteous manners won him esteem and renown. In August, 1793, Benjamin Randall, visited the town and baptized a number. Finally, becoming deeply interested and zealous, Brother Young was ordained on June 28, 1796, by a council from the Yearly Meeting consisting of Whitney, Buzzell, Randall, Boody and others. He then entered upon a useful pastorate of thirty-five years. In 1798 he baptized thirty in Canterbury. In 1800, a remarkable interest sprang up chiefly through his labors at New Hampton. A church of sixty-four members was organized there by him on Jan. 6th, and for eight months, the glorious work continued, till 114 had been baptized and added to the church, "all or chiefly by our dear and precious brother, Elder Winthrop Young" as Elder Randall, who was present at the last baptism, makes the record. Possessing worldly means, he was benevolent and humble. He was of strong mind and large heart. His deep voice presented petitions in public prayer in such a way that Randall was heard to say, "We have no man among us that can pray like Brother Young." In 1822 at the age of nearly seventy, he was still active, baptizing a number at Northfield. In 1829, Rev. John Harrison was chosen as assistant pastor at Canterbury. Rev. Young died in the 80th year of his age.

Rev Zebina Young
Birth:
Dec. 15, 1795
New Hampshire
Death:
Dec. 24, 1874
New Hampshire
Burial:
Elmwood Cemetery
Franconia
Grafton County, New Hampshire

He was licensed to preach at Lisbon, 1829 and ordained there Dec. 29, 1831. His pastorates were in New Hampshire, Vermont and Canada.